Application Guide for AFINCH (Analysis of Flows in Networks of Channels) Described by NHDPlus

By David J. Holtschlag

National Water Availability and Use Program—Great Lakes Basin Pilot

Scientific Investigations Report 2009–5188

U.S. Department of the Interior
U.S. Geological Survey

U.S. Department of the Interior
KEN SALAZAR, Secretary

U.S. Geological Survey
Suzette M. Kimball, Acting Director

U.S. Geological Survey, Reston, Virginia: 2009

For more information on the USGS—the Federal source for science about the Earth, its natural and living resources, natural hazards, and the environment, visit http://www.usgs.gov or call 1-888-ASK-USGS

For an overview of USGS information products, including maps, imagery, and publications, visit http://www.usgs.gov/pubprod

To order this and other USGS information products, visit http://store.usgs.gov

Suggested citation:
Holtschlag, D.J., 2009, Application guide for AFINCH (analysis of flows in networks of channels) described by NHDPlus: U.S. Geological Survey Scientific Investigations Report 2009-5188, 106 p.

Preface

This report describes the initial development of a U.S. Geological Survey program for Analysis of Flows in Networks of Channels (AFINCH) described by the National Hydrography Dataset (NHDPlus). The performance of the program has been tested in only limited applications. Further development and testing of the code is anticipated.

Contents

Contents—Continued

Contents—Continued

Figures

Figures—Continued

Tables

Conversion Factors and List of Symbols

Inch/Pound to SI

Multiply	By	To obtain
Length		
inch (in.)	2.54	centimeter (cm)
foot (ft)	0.3048	meter (m)
mile (mi)	1.609	kilometer (km)
Area		
acre	0.4047	hectare (ha)
acre	0.004047	square kilometer (km^2)
square foot (ft^2)	0.0929	square meter (m^2)
square mile (mi^2)	259	hectare (ha)
square mile (mi^2)	2.590	square kilometer (km^2)
Volume		
gallon (gal)	0.003785	cubic meter (m^3)
cubic foot (ft^3)	0.02832	cubic meter (m^3)
acre-foot (acre-ft)	1,233	cubic meter (m^3)
Flow rate		
foot per second (ft/s)	0.3048	meter per second (m/s)
cubic foot per second (ft^3/s)	0.02832	cubic meter per second (m^3/s)
cubic foot per second per square mile [(ft^3/s)/mi^2]	0.01093	cubic meter per second per square
kilometer [(m^3/s)/km^2] gallon per minute (gal/min)	0.06309	liter per second (L/s)
million gallons per day (Mgal/d)	0.04381	cubic meter per second (m^3/s)
mile per hour (mi/h)	1.609	kilometer per hour (km/h)
Mass		
pound, avoirdupois (lb)	0.4536	kilogram (kg)
ton, short (2,000 lb)	0.9072	megagram (Mg)
ton, long (2,240 lb)	1.016	megagram (Mg)

Temperature in degrees Celsius (°C) may be converted to degrees Fahrenheit (°F) as follows:

$$°F=(1.8×°C)+32$$

Temperature in degrees Fahrenheit (°F) may be converted to degrees Celsius (°C) as follows:

$$°C=(°F-32)/1.8$$

List of Symbols

Symbol	Name
$\{S\}$	Brackets indicate a set, here the set S.
$\{s \subset S\}$	The set operator indicates a subset, here the set s is a subset of S.
$|s|$	For a set s, the set operator $|s|$ indicates the number of elements in the set.
$\subseteq ComID_{is}$	For $ComID_{is}$ as the unique identifier of the flowline on which streamgage *is* is located, the set operator $\subseteq$ identifies the set of $ComID$ (flowlines) on or upstream of $ComID_{is}$.
$\cap ComID_{is}$	The set operator $\cap$ indicates the intersection of ComIDs at streamgage is with all ComIDs upstream of all upstream gages.
$\Delta A_{s_{iy}}$	Indicates a vector of incremental drainage areas at stations s during the iy^{th} year. Incremental drainage area is the drainage area at the streamgage minus the drainage area monitored by any upstream gage. Thus, $\Delta A_{s_{iy}} = N_{iy}^{-1} \cdot A_{s_{iy}}$, where $A_{s_{iy}}$ is a vector of drainage areas at active streamgages in the iy^{th} year.
$\hat{\beta}$	An estimated vector of regression parameters for estimating water yields.
$\varepsilon_{iy,im}$	A vector of regression errors for the iy^{th} year and im^{th} month.
N_{iy}	Indicates the network design matrix for year iy. The network design matrix is a lower triangular matrix of zeros and ones, which has dimension equal to the number of streamgages operated in the iy year. Streamgages are represented by ones in rows and columns within the matrix, where streamgages are in downstream order.
$\Delta Q_{s_{iy}}$	Indicates a vector of incremental monthly streamflow at stations s during the iy^{th} year. Incremental streamflow is the streamflow at the streamgage minus the streamflow monitored by any upstream gage. Thus, $\Delta Q_{s_{iy}} = N_{iy}^{-1} \cdot Q_{s_{iy}}$, where is a vector of streamflows at active streamgages in the iy^{th} year.
X	X indicates the regression design matrix, which includes columns for explanatory climatic data and basin characteristics augmented by a leading column of ones.
$\Delta Y_{s_{iy}}$	Indicates a vector of incremental monthly water yields at stations s during the iy^{th} year. Incremental water yield is the water yield is the element wise quotiet of incremental streamflow divided by incremental drainage area. A prime symbol is used to distinguish between water yields that have been adjusted for specified water uses.
$Z_{iy,im}$	The smoothed estimate of flow in year iy for month im.

Application Guide for AFINCH (Analysis of Flows in Networks of Channels) Described by NHDPlus

By David J. Holtschlag

Abstract

AFINCH (Analysis of Flows in Networks of CHannels) is a computer application that can be used to generate a time series of monthly flows at stream segments (flowlines) and water yields for catchments defined in the National Hydrography Dataset Plus (NHDPlus) value-added attribute system. AFINCH provides a basis for integrating monthly flow data from streamgages, water-use data, monthly climatic data, and land-cover characteristics to estimate natural monthly water yields from catchments by user-defined regression equations. Images of monthly water yields for active streamgages are generated in AFINCH and provide a basis for detecting anomalies in water yields, which may be associated with undocumented flow diversions or augmentations. Water yields are multiplied by the drainage areas of the corresponding catchments to estimate monthly flows. Flows from catchments are accumulated downstream through the streamflow network described by the stream segments. For stream segments where streamgages are active, ratios of measured to accumulated flows are computed. These ratios are applied to upstream water yields to proportionally adjust estimated flows to match measured flows. Flow is conserved through the NHDPlus network. A time series of monthly flows can be generated for stream segments that average about 1-mile long, or monthly water yields from catchments that average about 1 square mile. Estimated monthly flows can be displayed within AFINCH, examined for nonstationarity, and tested for monotonic trends. Monthly flows also can be used to estimate flow-duration characteristics at stream segments. AFINCH generates output files of monthly flows and water yields that are compatible with ArcMap, a geographical information system analysis and display environment. Chloropleth maps of monthly water yield and flow can be generated and analyzed within ArcMap by joining NHDPlus data structures with AFINCH output. Matlab code for the AFINCH application is presented.

Introduction

Multiple regression analysis (MRA) commonly is used to develop equations for estimating mean monthly flows and monthly flow-duration characteristics at ungaged stream sites on the basis of climatic and basin characteristics (Hamilton and others, 2008). Despite widespread use, multiple regression estimates of streamflow characteristics have limitations. First, MRA estimates do not conserve flow in a network, so that the sum of flows estimated for individual contributing areas generally does not equal the flow estimated for the area as a whole. Second, estimated flow characteristics do not match measured flow characteristics at streamgages. Thus, reconciling flow characteristics estimated from data at one or more nearby streamgages with regression estimates can be problematic. Third, streamflow records known to be affected by water use are commonly excluded from the analysis, but streamflow records with unknown water use effects may be mistakenly included. Fourth, streamflow and climatic characteristics are assumed to be stationary throughout the period of record used in the analysis. Thus, streamflow records for different time periods, which may have trends and differ in their flow-variability characteristics, may be considered homogeneous when, in fact, they are not. Milly and others (2008) challenge the common assumption of stationarity in hydrologic data. AFINCH provides an alternative to MRA analysis when flow continuity, consistency with measured flow conditions, water-use effects, or effects of nonstationarity may be important.

AFINCH is a computer program, written in the Matlab programming language (The MathWorks, 2008a), for estimating time series of monthly flows and water yields. Monthly streamflow data at active streamgages adjusted for upstream water use, monthly climatic data, and land-cover characteristics provide a basis for developing regression equations to estimate natural monthly water yields at individual catchments. These water yields are multiplied by drainage areas of the associated catchments to compute monthly flows. These flows are accumulated downstream through the streamflow network and compared with measured flows. On stream segments (flowlines) where active streamgages occur, ratios of measured to accumulated flows are computed. These ratios are applied to upstream water yields so that resulting flows are constrained to match measured flows.

The United States is divided into hydrologic units based on surface drainage features (U.S. Geological Survey, 2008). A hierarchical Hydrologic Unit Code (HUC) is formed to identify a more refined level of subdivision by appending a 2-digit code onto the end of the code identifying the previous level. In particular, the coding system divides the United States into 21 regions (2 digits) (fig. 1), 221 subregions (4 digits), 378 accounting units (6 digits), and 2,264 cataloguing units (8 digits). Locally, this process has been extended to define 10-digit watersheds, 12-digit subwatersheds, 14-digit catchments, and 16-digit subcatchments.

The NHDPlus system subdivides hydrologic units into catchments. NHDPlus data, which are generally distributed by hydrologic regions, define catchment areas that are bounded by watersheds. Within a hydrologic region, each catchment is represented by a polygon and is uniquely identified by a numeric Grid_Code. For example, the 118,000 square miles (mi^2) area that drains largely from the U.S. part of the Great Lakes basin (hydrologic region 04) (fig. 1) is represented by 104,343 catchments. The average size of these catchments is 1.13 mi^2, the smallest catchment is less than 0.001 mi^2, and the largest U.S. catchment is 105 mi^2.

This report describes the application of the AFINCH (Analysis of Flows in Networks of CHannels) model to estimate time series of monthly water yields from catchments and flows at stream segments defined as flowlines within the NHDPlus geospatial surface-water framework. The U.S. portion of the Great Lakes basin (hydrologic region 04) within hydrologic subregion 0405, referred to as the Southeast Lake Michigan, is used to describe NHDPlus characteristics, demonstrate the AFINCH application, and provide preliminary estimates of flows and water yields from 1971 to 2000. Data file formats for input of monthly streamflow, water-use, and climatic data are described. Processing steps in AFINCH are discussed, and formats for output datasets are presented. This report assumes user proficiency with NHDPlus, developed by the U.S. Environmental Protection Agency (USEPA) and the U.S. Geological Survey (USGS); Matlab, a computation, visualization, and programming environment developed by The Mathworks, Inc.; and ArcMap, the geographical information systems (GIS) program developed by Environmental Systems Research Institute (ESRI).

Selected catchment attributes are predefined within NHDPlus, including attributes derived from the 1992 National Land Cover Dataset (NLCD). NLCD was the first nationally (conterminously) consistent land-cover mapping project in the United States. AFINCH uses the surface-water topology and value-added attributes defined in NHDPlus (NHDPlus User Guide, 2008) to analyze flows in networks of channels. NHDPlus provides a nationally consistent basis for these geospatial analyses. For each NHDPlus catchment, percentages of NLCD classes described as Water areas are coded as either Open Water (11) or Perennial Ice and Snow (12); Developed areas as Low Intensity Residential (21), High Intensity Residential (22), or Commercial / Industrial / Transportation (23); Barren areas as Bare Rock / Sand / Clay (31), Quarries / Strip Mines / Gravel Pits (32), and Transitional (33); Forested Upland areas as Deciduous Forest (41), Evergreen Forest (42), or Mixed Forest (43); Shrubland areas as Shrubland (51); Non-natural woody areas as Orchards, Vineyards, and other areas maintained for the production of fruits, nuts, berries, or ornamentals (61); Herbaceous Upland areas as Grasslands / Herbaceous (71); Planted / Cultivated areas as Pasture / Hay (81), Row Crops (82), Small Grains (83), Fallow (84), and Urban / Recreational Grasses (85); Wetland areas as Woody Wetlands (91); and Emergent Herbaceous Wetlands (92).

For this report, average monthly air temperature and total precipitation data were computed for each year in the period 1970-2000 and for all catchments in hydrologic subregion 0405, which includes parts of the following 8 states: Michigan, Wisconsin, Minnesota, Illinois, Indiana, Ohio, Pennsylvania, and New York (fig. 1). The climatic data are based on 2.5 arc-minute (approximately 4 kilometers) grids of PRISM (Parameter-elevation Regressions on Independent Slopes Model) data by Daly and Taylor (1998a,b). PRISM monthly temperature and precipitation datasets are available from 1895 to 2008.

NHDPlus links stream segments (flowlines) to catchments and to other flowlines. Flowlines include streams and rivers, canals and ditches, pipelines, artificial paths, coastlines, and connectors. The topology of flowlines defined within NHDPlus provides a mechanism to accumulate flows from catchments and route flows through a drainage network. In AFINCH, water use, including withdrawals, augmentations, and diversions, also can be associated with flowlines and accounted for along with catchment flows.

Within NHDPlus, one or more streamgages may be located at different points along a single flowline. In AFINCH, however, data from a single active streamgage may be associated with an individual flowline. Where multiple active streamgages occur on a flowline, the AFINCH user selects the streamgage that best represents flow conditions.

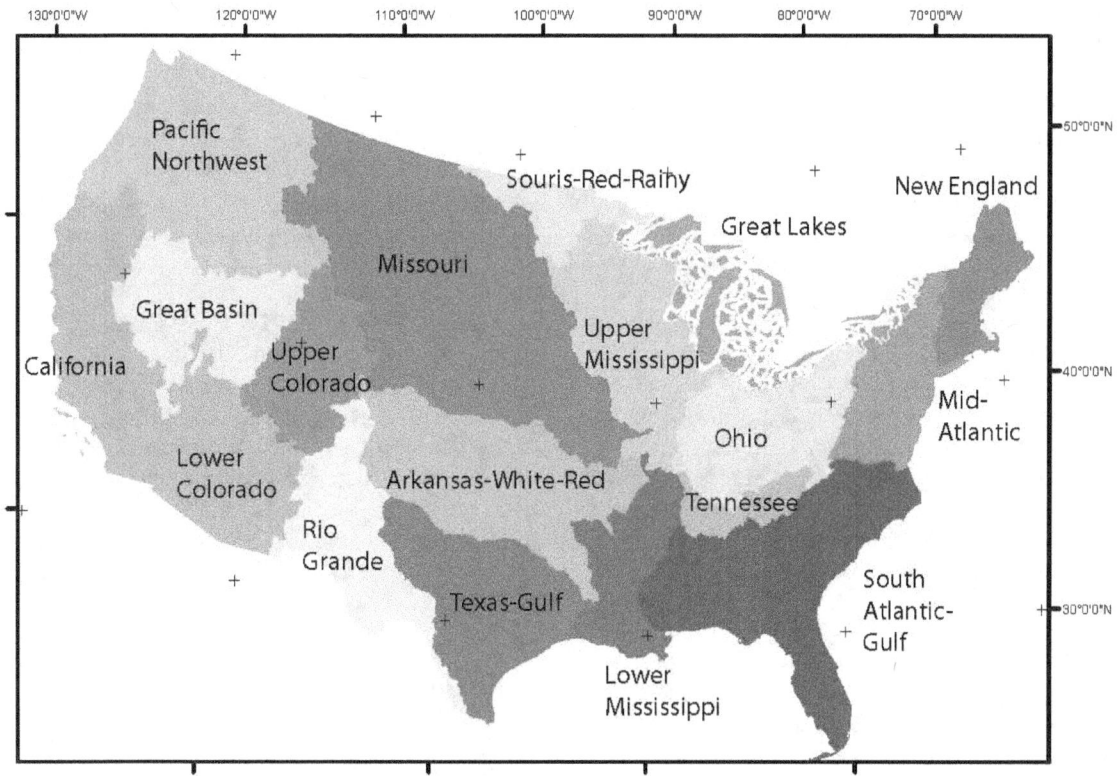

Figure 1. Hydrologic regions in the conterminous United States with designated names.

Monthly flows at streamgages, adjusted for specified water uses, can be used to compute average monthly water yields at upstream catchments that form the basins of the streamgages. These water yields can be related to the NLCD land cover and climatic characteristics defined for the basin through multiple regression analysis. The regression relations can then be used to estimate water yields from individual catchments and compute corresponding flows at all flowlines in the network. For flowlines where flow is gaged, estimated flows can be constrained to match measured flows (adjusted for water use) by adjusting water yields at upstream catchments by the ratio of measured to estimated flows. Estimated flows are unconstrained at ungaged flowlines, although specified water-use components are applied. The time series of monthly flows provides a basis for trend and flow-duration analysis at any flowline in the NHDPlus network for the user to assess stationarity.

Methods and Data Used in AFINCH Modeling

AFINCH uses topological information from NHDPlus, monthly precipitation and air temperature data, monthly streamflow data at streamgages, and water-use data at streams derived from cooperative programs between State and local governmental agencies and the USGS. A brief overview of how each component is used in the analysis follows.

NHDPlus Constructs and Data

NHDPlus is an integrated suite of application-ready geospatial data products that includes features from the National Hydrography Dataset (U.S. Geological Survey, 2009), the National Elevation Dataset (http://ned.usgs.gov/), and the National Watershed Boundary Dataset (Natural Resources Conservation Service, 2009), (U.S. Environmental Protection Agency and U.S. Geological Survey, 2008). NHDPlus includes a stream network based on the medium resolution (1:100,000 scale) NHD, connectivity within the stream network and to associated catchments, feature naming, and a set of value-added attributes (VAA). Catchments initially were delineated on the basis of the 30-meter (m) digital elevation model (DEM), but were modified for consistency with the certified watershed boundaries, where available. The VAAs provide the basis for navigation through the streamflow network, controlling the level of detail in displays, and GIS modeling.

NHDPlus data are distributed by hydrologic region (fig. 1). Data for most hydrologic regions in the United States can be downloaded by following the instructions at the NHDPlus data Web site (Horizon Systems Corporation, n.d.). The NHDPlus User Guide describes the versioning system, the directory structure, and data components.

The geospatial data terminology developed for NHDPlus is used extensively in the description of corresponding elements in AFINCH. This report attempts to maintain consistent terminology between AFINCH and NHDPlus. A brief overview of this specialized terminology is presented, although it is discussed in greater detail in the NHDPlus User Guide (U.S. Environmental Protection Agency and U.S. Geological Survey, 2008).

The geospatial data components that make up NHDPlus can be categorized as feature classes or attribute tables. A feature class is a collection of geographic features with the same geometry type (such as points, lines, or polygons), the same attributes, and the same spatial reference. Feature classes can be stored in shapefiles or grids. A shapefile is a vector data storage format for storing the location, shape, and attributes of geographic features, such as stream segments. Grids are groups of cells formed by the intersections of vertical and horizontal lines spaced 30-meters apart superimposed on a map with a spatial reference. An attribute table is a database table containing information about a set of geographic features arranged so that each row represents a feature and each column represents an attribute. In attribute tables or lists derived from attribute tables, observations in rows are referred to as records, and attributes in columns are referred to as fields. NHDPlus geospatial datasets used in AFINCH are described in the following paragraphs.

NHDFlowline Shapefile

The NHDFlowline shapefile describes waterway elements that include segments of streams, rivers, canals, ditches, pipelines, artificial paths, coastlines, and connectors, which generally are referred to as flowlines. Flowlines are displayed as one or more georeferenced line segment in GIS software, such as ESRI's ArcMap. The graphical depictions are linked to an attribute table, which uses the dBase file

structure that is an industry standard for storing related data in a binary file format. The attribute table contains a unique identifier for each flowline (*ComID*), the length of the flowline in kilometers (*LengthKM*), and the reach code (*ReachCode*), a 14-digit character string that describes the hydrologic unit (basin) associated with the flowline. NHDPlus reaches include one or more adjacent flowlines that have the same *ReachCode*. Flowlines are constructed through features such as lakes, ponds, reservoirs, and marshes to represent flow pathways throughout the stream network.

For example, in the U.S. Great Lakes basin (hydrologic region 04), there are 113,247 flowlines in the NHDFlowline (shapefile). The distribution of flowline lengths is right skewed with an average length of 1.17 mi, a minimum length of less than 0.001 mi, and a maximum length of 27.8 mi (mi). About 99 percent of the flowlines are less than 13.4 mi long. Within the flowline table, 92,809 unique *ReachCodes* identify reaches made up of one or more flowlines. Reaches are expected to remain unchanged with the resolution of the NHDPlus, while flowlines may change.

NHDFlowlineVAA Attribute Table

NHDFlowlineVAA is an attribute table that provides VAAs for each flowline. Attributes used in AFINCH include (1) the hydrologic sequence number (the integer field *Hydroseq* in the attribute table), (2) the integer from-node (*FromNode*) and to-node (*ToNode*) fields indicating the flow direction of a flowline, (3) the headwater indicator flag (*StartFlag*), and (4) a flag to indicate whether the flowline is a branch of a flowline that split into two or more flowlines (*Divergence*). *Hydroseq* is a nationally unique sequence number that places each flowline in hydrologic sequence. At any flowline, all upstream flowlines have higher hydrologic sequence numbers and all downstream flowlines have lower hydrologic sequence numbers. The *FromNode* and *ToNode* identifiers are unique numbers for virtual node endpoints of flowlines. A *StartFlag* value of "0" indicates that the flowline is not a headwater flowline, and a value of "1" indicates that the flowline is a headwater flowline. *Divergence* takes on a value of "0" if the flowline is not part of a divergence, a value of "1" if the flowline is the main path of a divergence, and a value of "2" if the flowline is a minor path of a divergence.

StreamGageEvent Shapefile

The NHDPlus StreamGageEvent is a shapefile that locates USGS streamgages along flowlines. A USGS streamgage is uniquely identified by its station number, which is contained in the field *Source_fea* of the associated attribute table. The streamgage flowline is identified by the field *ComID*, and the field *Measure* describes the distance to the station along the flowline from the downstream limit, as a percentage. Other fields of data in the StreamGageEvent table include the station name, drainage area at the gage, the latitude and longitude of the gage, and streamflow and streamflow-record characteristics. In the U.S. Great Lakes basin (hydrologic region 04), for example, 1,058 streamgages are identified.

Catchment Shapefiles

The NHDPlus catchment shapefile contains polygons outlining catchment boundaries. Defined attributes for catchments include the unique identifier *Grid_code*, the area of the catchment in square kilometers (*AreaSqKm*), and the number of 30-m square cells contained within the catchments (*Grid_Count*). Each catchment is uniquely associated with a flowline through the *ComID* field. Some flowlines, such as those used to connect with other flowlines through a waterbody represented by a polygon, however, do not have an associated catchment. For example, in the U.S. Great Lakes region, 104,343 catchments are defined, 8,904 fewer than the number of flowlines in the region. The average size of catchments is 1.13 mi^2, the smallest catchment is less than 0.001 mi^2, and the largest catchment is 294 mi^2, which is entirely within Ontario, Canada. The largest catchment within Hydrologic Region 04 in the United States is 105 mi^2, which is in Michigan's Lower Peninsula.

National Land Cover Data

The NHDPlus CatchmentAttributesNLCD file is an attribute table that contains the percentages of 21 land-cover categories described by the NLCD in the catchment. The fields are named "*NLCD_##*", where "##" represents a two-digit number associated with the land-cover category. The 21 categories are grouped under more broadly defined land-cover classes including water, developed, barren, forested land, shrub land, non-natural woody, herbaceous upland natural or semi-natural vegetation, herbaceous planted or cultivated, and wetlands. Percentages of these categories pertain only to the part of the catchment within the United States, but are computed as a percentage of the total area. Thus, any non-zero percentages in the fields *PCT_CN* (percentage in Canada) or *PCT_MX* (percentage in Mexico) must be added to the percentages in the NLCD to account for the entire catchment area (U.S. Environmental Protection Agency and U.S. Geological Survey, 2008). Each catchment is identified by its *Grid_code* and associated flowline by its *ComID*. Consistent with the catchment shapefile, there are 104,343 records in the CatchmentAttributesNLCD attribute table within subregion 04.

Monthly Data

AFINCH uses monthly streamflow, water-use, and climatic data to compute monthly streamflows at flowlines and water yields from catchments. Time series of monthly streamflow values were computed from data obtained through the USGS cooperative streamgaging program and formatted for input to AFINCH. Water-use information from various public and private agencies is compiled by the USGS (U.S. Geological Survey, 2009). In this study, monthly total precipitation and minimum and maximum air temperatures were obtained from the PRISM Group[1] (Oregon State University, 2008).

Streamflow Data

Monthly data for all stations monitored in a hydrologic subregion are grouped in individual ASCII (American Standard Code for Information Interchange) files by water year[2] and located in a relative subdirectory associated with the hydrologic subregion of interest. For example, monthly flows for all streamgages operated in hydrologic subregion 0405 during water year 2000 were included in the relative subdirectory '..\HSR0405\Streamflow' in a file named "ComIDStationDAMoAnQ2000.dat."

Data for each streamgaging station is contained in a single line (record), and records are arranged by increasing station number. Consistent with the file naming convention, the 16 tab-delimited fields within each record are (1) the *ComID* identifying the flowline on which the specific streamgage is located, (2) the USGS streamgage number, (3) the National Water Information System (NWIS) estimate of the drainage area at the streamgage in square miles, (4-15) monthly flows beginning with October of the calendar year prior to the water year and ending with September of the water year, and (16) the annual mean flow. All flows are in cubic feet per second.

Water-Use Information

Monthly water-use data also are stored in ASCII files and are located in a relative subdirectory associated with the hydrologic subregion number under study. For example, water-use data for hydrologic subregion 0405 are located in subdirectory '..\HSR0405\Wateruse' in a file named *ComID_WU_All.dat*. Each record in the water-use data file contains 13 tab-delimited fields, which represent the location and monthly water-use values at a particular flowline. The first

---

[1] PRISM Group, formerly Spatial Climate Analysis Service, was established at Oregon State University, Corvallis, Oregon, to provide climate related services and products. Dr. Christopher Daly is the director.

[2] Water year is the 12-month period from October 1 to September 30 and is identified by the year in which the period ends. October 1, 1970, to September 30, 1971, is the 1971 water year.

field is the *ComID*, identifying the flowline where the water use is occurring, and the remaining 12 fields are the monthly water-use values, beginning with October of the water year. Additional records are used to represent water use at other flowlines. Water withdrawals are indicated by negative water-use values, and flow augmentations are indicated by positive water-use values. All flows are in cubic feet per second.

In the initial development of AFINCH, time series of water-use data were not available for hydrologic subregion 0405. Therefore, a single test water-use data file, ComID_WU_All.dat, was used for all water years. In the future, it is anticipated that this file will be populated with water-use data and made year dependent, following the convention used for streamflow data, such as *"ComID_WU_2000.dat."*

Climatic Data

Monthly total precipitation and minimum and maximum air temperature data were obtained from grids of data downloaded from the PRISM Group. Grids of monthly precipitation, temperature, and dew point are available beginning with January 1895. Provisional climatic data usually are available within 30 days of the end of the current month. Distribution of climatic data after June 2008 has been suspended, however, because of insufficient funding (http://www.prism.oregonstate.edu/). If updating is not resumed, an alternative source of monthly climatic data will be needed for future analyses. In AFINCH, grids of climatic data are overlain with polygons representing catchment boundaries to estimate spatially averaged precipitation and temperature values. The average of the minimum and maximum temperature values was used to estimate the average monthly temperature.

AFINCH Code

AFINCH is coded in the Matlab programming language and requires the Matlab environment (version 7.8, R2009a or later) and the Statistics Toolbox (v. 7.1 or later). AFINCH was developed on a personal computer running the Microsoft Windows XP operating system. The code is modularized into scripts and functions. Graphical user interfaces (GUI) were developed to facilitate input to and control of AFINCH. Graphical and textual outputs are generated to facilitate interpretation and document the results of the analyses. AFINCH code is expected to be in a subdirectory that is on the path of directories searched by Matlab. To add a subdirectory to the search path, left click on the Matlab's File menu, select "Set Path..." from the dropdown list, select the "Add Folder..." option, browse to the subdirectory containing the AFINCH code, and left-click the button labeled "OK" near the bottom right of the window.

Matlab code is interpreted rather than compiled, so it is stored in ASCII files that contain a descriptive name beginning with "AF" for the filename prefix and the standard extension "m" for the filename suffix. Matlab files commonly are referred to as M-files. There are two types of M-files: scripts and functions. Script M-files operate on variables in a common memory area referred to as the Matlab workspace. Functions M-files have a local memory allocation, but can accept input and output arguments and can access variables in the workspace through function calls. For those familiar with the Matlab programming language, AFINCH code is straightforward to read and modify for specialized requirements. The primary modules are discussed in the following sections.

The generalized description of the AFINCH code provided in this report is intended to provide a conceptual understanding of the processing steps used in the AFINCH analysis rather than a detailed description of the data structures and algorithms underlying the AFINCH code. The AFINCH code is provided as an appendix, however, for the interested reader.

Directory Structure and Contents

Input and output files for AFINCH are arranged in a hierarchical set of directories that are accessed by relative addressing as shown in figure 2. The top directory, "AFinch," can occur anywhere within the computer's directory system. Once the input files are created, the analyst is expected to initiate AFINCH in the AWork subdirectory, one level below the top (AFinch) directory. Matlab code for AFINCH may be stored below the MLCode subdirectory in a subdirectory labeled according to the current AFINCH version (Ver##).

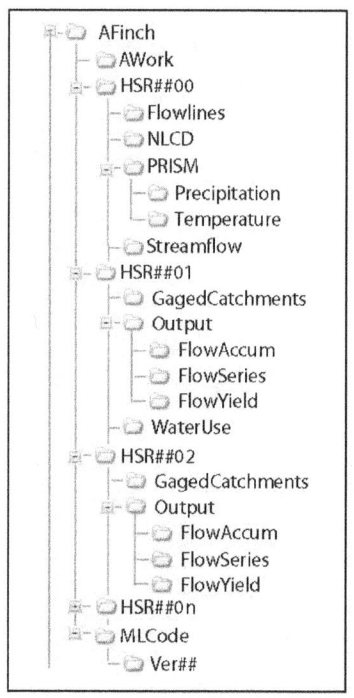

Figure 2. Computer directory structure expected for relative file addressing in AFINCH. (HSR means Hydrologic Sub Region. For example, HSR##02 would refer to the second hydrologic subregion in the hydrologic region generically referenced by the two-digit code ##).

HSR##00 Directory

The directory HSR##00 refers to the two-digit hydrologic region that includes data common to all four-digit hydrologic subregions being analyzed. The hydrologic region subdirectory contains four primary subdirectories that contain input files: Flowlines, NLCD, PRISM, and Streamflow. The contents of the subdirectories are discussed subsequently.

Flowlines Subdirectory

The ..\HSR##00\Flowlines subdirectory is expected to contain the file "nhdflowline.txt." This ASCII file can be created by export from ArcMap using the attribute table associated with the NHDPlus##\hydrography\nhdflowline (shapefile), where ## designates the two-digit hydrologic region of interest. (In this report, all subdirectories with the top-level directory NHDPlus## reference files distributed through the NHDPlus system.) The nhdflowline.txt file contains three comma-separated columns of data from the attribute file: *ComID* (uniquely identifying the flowline), *LengthKm* (indicating the length of the flowline in kilometers), and *ReachCode* (identifying the location of the flowline in the hydrologic region). A header row identifies the contents of each column, but is not read by AFINCH. The ndhflowline.txt file for hydrologic region 04, contains 113,249 rows of data. An excerpt of the nhdflowline.txt file is shown in figure 3.

NLCD National Land Cover Data Subdirectory

The NLCD subdirectory is expected to contain the file "catchmentattributesnlcd.txt." This file can be generated from ArcMap by exporting the contents of ..\NHDPlus##\catchmentattributesnlcd.dbf file as a text file ("txt" filename extension) with comma- separated values. The catchmentattributesnlcd.txt file for hydrologic region 04 contained 26 comma-delimited columns and 104,344 rows of data including the *ComID* associated with the catchment, the *Grid_code* uniquely identifying the catchment, and percentages of each NLCD data type. An excerpt of the data file is shown in figure 4.

```
C:\Projects\Water Availability\Analysis\AFinch\HSR0400\Flowlines\nhdflowline.txt
COMID,LENGTHKM,REACHCODE¶
271811,0.084000,04030112000113¶
271813,0.520000,04030112000111¶
271815,4.492000,04030112000057¶
271817,1.764000,04030112000115¶
271819,0.552000,04030112000109¶
271821,0.695000,04030112000056¶
271823,2.091000,04030112000108¶
271825,2.554000,04030112000108¶
```

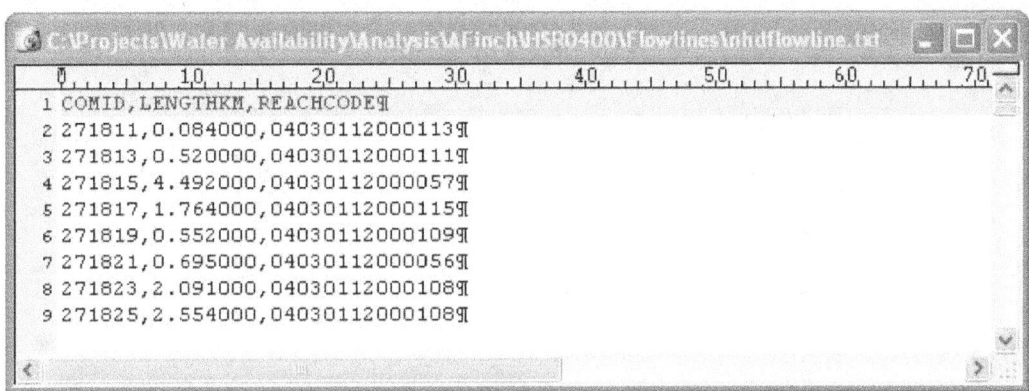

Figure 3. Excerpt of the contents of the nhdflowline.txt file for hydrologic region 04.

```
C:\Projects\Water Availability\Analysis\AFinch\HSR0400\NLCD\catchmentattributesnlcd.txt*
"COMID","GRID_CODE","NLCD_11","NLCD_12","NLCD_21","NLCD_22","NLCD_23","NLCD_31","NLCD_3
12936664,2052588,0.137420,0,5.313790,0.137420,0.847450,0,0,0,30.989460,1.145210,0.75584
12936666,2052589,6.521740,0,0,0,0,0,0,43.478260,0,0,0,0,0,50,0,0,0,0,0,0,100¶
12936668,2052590,0,0,0,0,0,0,0,0,0,0,0,0,5.416670,94.583340,0,0,0,0,0,0,100¶
12936670,2052591,0,0,6.604570,0.423370,4.995770,0,0,0,37.256560,4.826420,1.354780,0,0,0,
12936672,2052592,0,0,0,0,0,0,0,0,0,0,0,0,4.576660,95.423340,0,0,0,0,0,0,100¶
12936674,2052593,0.545200,0,0.545200,0,0,0,0,0,18.537030,0.590640,0.181730,0,0,0,14.084
12936676,2052594,0.271690,0,9.077830,5.657660,5.417930,0,0,0,7.831230,0.511420,0.239730,
12936678,2052595,0.392540,0,0.147200,0,0,0,0,0,25.956820,1.373900,0.098130,0,0,0,2.7968
```

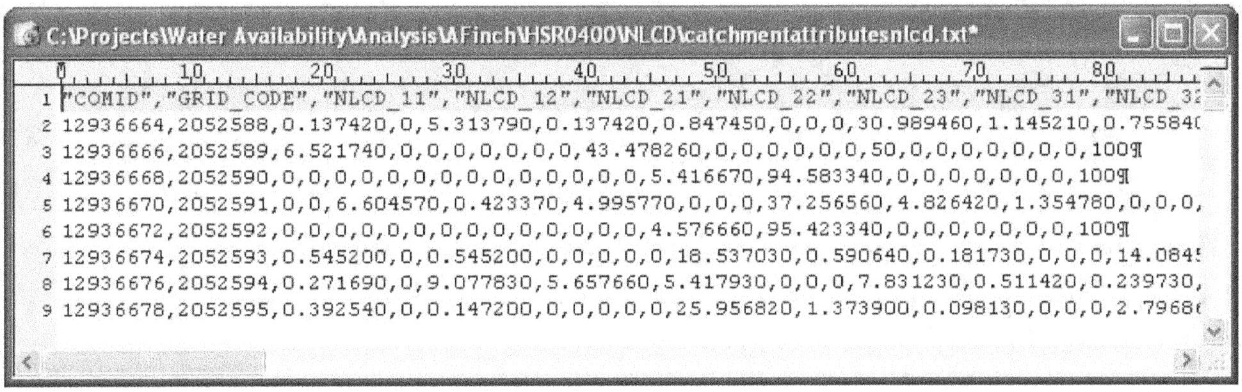

Figure 4. Excerpt of the catchmentattributesnlcd.txt file for hydrologic region 04.

PRISM Subdirectory

The PRISM directory contains two subdirectories, Precipitation and Temperature, which are expected to contain spatially averaged, monthly climatic data for each catchment in the hydrologic region. Total precipitation and average air temperature data for each water year are stored in separate sets of files. For preliminary analysis of hydrologic region 04, the spatial averages were computed by intersecting square 30-m cells describing specific catchment areas as the zone grid, with square 2.5-arcmin cells of PRISM climatic information as the data grid using the zonal statistics function in ArcMap. The expected format and file naming conventions of the climatic data files are discussed in the following paragraphs.

Precipitation. The file naming convention for monthly precipitation data is "PrismPrecipWYyyyy.dat," where the four-digit water year under analysis replaces the four "y" placeholders. The precipitation data files are expected to have a four-line header indicating the corresponding column contents. AFINCH does not read the header. Each remaining line contains the fields *Grid_code*, which uniquely identifies the catchment (*Grid_CodeP*), the drainage area of the catchment in square miles (*GCAreaSqMi*), 12 monthly precipitation values (in area inches for the water year beginning in October), and the total annual precipitation. Fields are delimited by one or more spaces. An excerpt of the precipitation data for hydrologic region 04 is shown in figure 5.

Temperature. The file naming convention for monthly temperature data is "PrismTempAveWYyyyy.dat," where the four-digit water year under analysis replaces the four "y" placeholders. A four-line header is used to identify the column contents, but is not read by AFINCH. The remaining lines contain the fields *Grid_code* for the corresponding catchment (*Grid_CodeT*) and 12 monthly values of the average of the monthly maximum and minimum air temperatures, in degrees Celsius (*TdC*). Fields are delimited by one or more spaces. An excerpt from a temperature file from hydrologic region 04 is shown in figure 6.

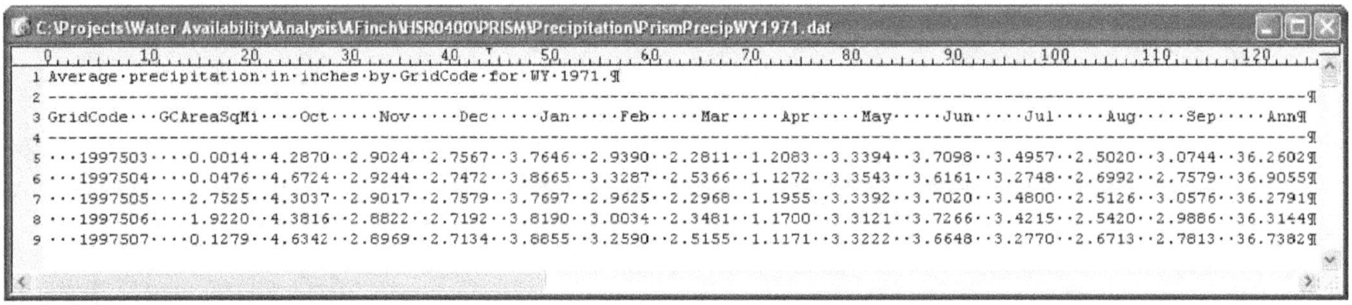
C:\Projects\Water Availability\Analysis\AFinch\HSR0400\PRISM\Precipitation\PrismPrecipWY1971.dat

```
Average precipitation in inches by GridCode for WY 1971.
------------------------------------------------------------------------------------------------------------------------
GridCode   GCAreaSqMi    Oct     Nov     Dec     Jan     Feb     Mar     Apr     May     Jun     Jul     Aug     Sep     Ann
------------------------------------------------------------------------------------------------------------------------
   1997503    0.0014  4.2870  2.9024  2.7567  3.7646  2.9390  2.2811  1.2083  3.3394  3.7098  3.4957  2.5020  3.0744  36.2602
   1997504    0.0476  4.6724  2.9244  2.7472  3.8665  3.3287  2.5366  1.1272  3.3543  3.6161  3.2748  2.6992  2.7579  36.9055
   1997505    2.7525  4.3037  2.9017  2.7579  3.7697  2.9625  2.2968  1.1955  3.3392  3.7020  3.4800  2.5126  3.0576  36.2791
   1997506    1.9220  4.3816  2.8822  2.7192  3.8190  3.0034  2.3481  1.1700  3.3121  3.7266  3.4215  2.5420  2.9886  36.3144
   1997507    0.1279  4.6342  2.8969  2.7134  3.8855  3.2590  2.5155  1.1171  3.3222  3.6648  3.2770  2.6713  2.7813  36.7382
```

Figure 5. Excerpt of the PRISM-based monthly precipitation file for hydrologic region 04.

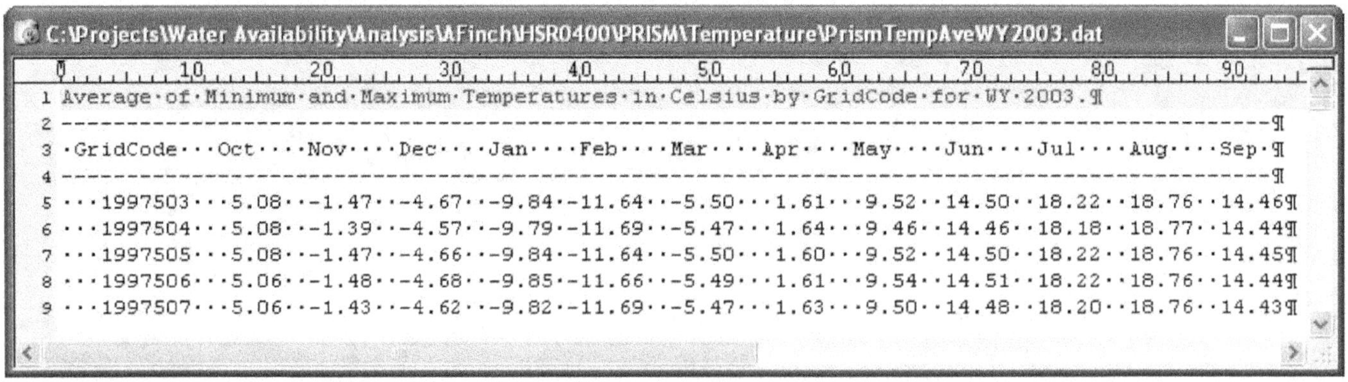
C:\Projects\Water Availability\Analysis\AFinch\HSR0400\PRISM\Temperature\PrismTempAveWY2003.dat

```
Average of Minimum and Maximum Temperatures in Celsius by GridCode for WY 2003.
-------------------------------------------------------------------------------------
 GridCode   Oct    Nov    Dec    Jan    Feb    Mar    Apr    May    Jun    Jul    Aug    Sep
-------------------------------------------------------------------------------------
   1997503   5.08  -1.47  -4.67  -9.84 -11.64  -5.50   1.61   9.52  14.50  18.22  18.76  14.46
   1997504   5.08  -1.39  -4.57  -9.79 -11.69  -5.47   1.64   9.46  14.46  18.18  18.77  14.44
   1997505   5.08  -1.47  -4.66  -9.84 -11.64  -5.50   1.60   9.52  14.50  18.22  18.76  14.45
   1997506   5.06  -1.48  -4.68  -9.85 -11.66  -5.49   1.61   9.54  14.51  18.22  18.76  14.44
   1997507   5.06  -1.43  -4.62  -9.82 -11.69  -5.47   1.63   9.50  14.48  18.20  18.76  14.43
```

Figure 6. Excerpt of a PRISM-based monthly temperature data file in hydrologic region 04.

Streamflow Subdirectory

The streamflow subdirectory is expected to contain files of monthly average streamflow data for all streamgages in the hydrologic subregion operated during the water year under analysis. The file naming convention follows the file contents as "ComIDStationDAMoAnQyyyy.dat." In particular, the single tab-delimited (») fields are the *ComID* of the flowline on which the gaging station is located, the (Station) number assigned to the streamgage, the basin drainage area at the streamgage (in square miles) as indicated by NWIS (AreaSqMi), monthly flow values (in cubic feet per second) for the water year beginning in October, and the annual mean streamflow (*Q*). The file is not expected to contain a header line. An excerpt of a file containing streamflow information is shown in figure 7.

Hydrologic Subregions (HSR####) Directories

AFINCH is applied to four-digit hydrologic subregions; therefore, a subdirectory is expected for each four-digit hydrologic subregion of interest in the hydrologic region.

In figure 2, a generic directory structure is illustrated for *nn* hydrologic subregions ##01, ##02, ..., ##*nn*. In this figure, the expanded subdirectory for HSR##01 shows the expected subdirectory structure common to all hydrologic subregions. The expected file contents of these subdirectories are discussed next.

GagedCatchments Subdirectory

The subdirectory GagedCatchments of the hydrologic subregion directories contains files for each streamgage included in the analysis. The file naming convention uses the USGS streamgage number as the filename prefix, and 'dat' as the filename suffix. USGS streamgage numbers commonly are eight-digit numbers that begin with the two-digit number of the hydrologic region. For example, USGS streamgage 04112500, Red Cedar River at East Lansing, Michigan, has a file in the GagedCatchments subdirectory named "04112500.dat" (fig. 8). Each streamgage file contains four fields delimited with one or more spaces: *Grid_code, ComID, AreaSqKm,* and *ReachCode.* A single header line in the file indicates the column contents.

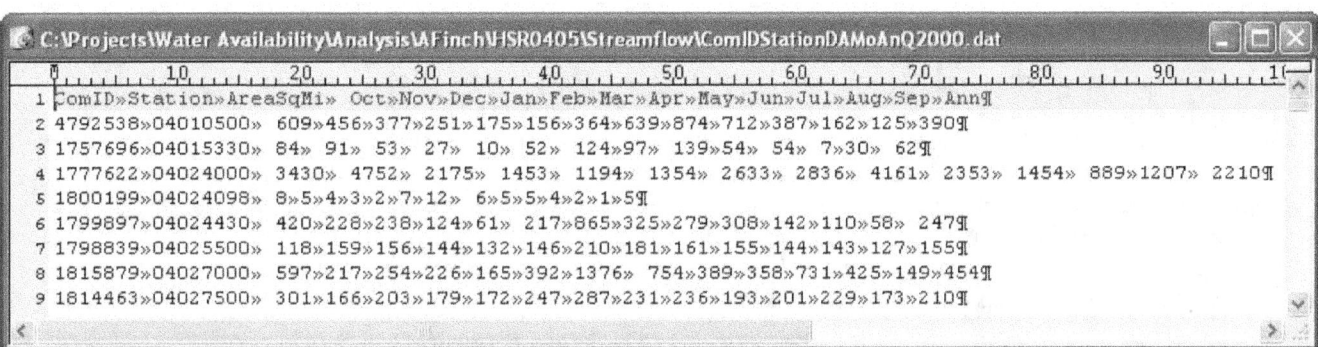

Figure 7. Excerpt of file containing monthly streamflow data in hydrologic region 04.

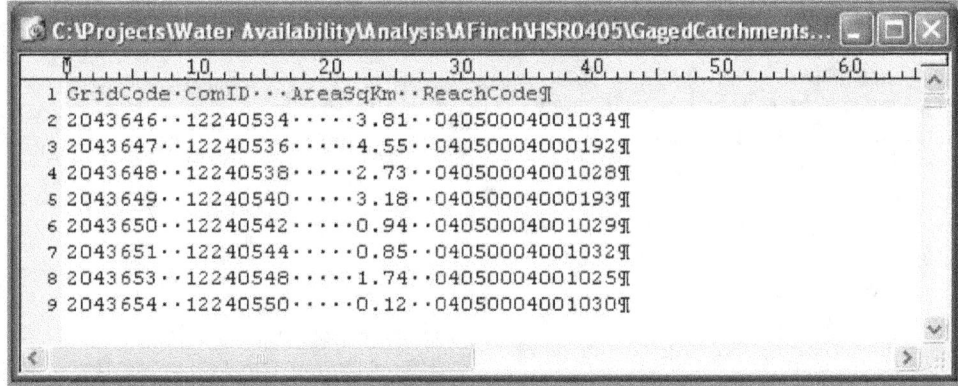

Figure 8. Excerpt of file containing catchment information for streamgage 04112500 on the Red Cedar River near East Lansing, Michigan.

The contents for each streamgage file were generated though the use of the Flow Table Navigator Tool in ArcMap. Specifically, the Navigator Tool was used to select all flowlines on or upstream from a flowline on which a gaging station was located, as indicated by the NHDPlus StreamGageEvent Layer. The selected flowlines were exported to a shapefile. The catchment shapefile was then joined to the Flowline shapefile for the selected streamgage. The two files were joined such that records in the catchment shapefile that did not have a *ComID* matching a *ComID* in the flowline shapefile were excluded. The four selected fields (*Grid_code*, *ComID*, *AreaSqKm*, and *ReachCode*) were then exported to an ASCII file to provide the data needed for the streamgage file used in AFINCH.

Running AFINCH

Once the Matlab application is launched and the working directory is set to "…AFinch\AWork," AFINCH can be initiated by typing "AFinch" into the Matlab command window after the prompt "≫." (Note that Matlab variables and commands are case sensitive.) In response, the script AFinch (appendix 1) runs and a question dialog box is presented to determine whether the user would like to continue a previous AFINCH session by loading variables from a saved workspace. If the user clicks on the 'Yes' button, an input dialogue box is presented for the user to enter the name of the AFINCH workspace saved previously. In anticipated future versions of AFINCH, loading a previously saved workspace will allow the user to avoid repeating some of the initial processing steps. The default of 'No,' which currently is the only option supported, requires the user to move sequentially through the processing steps.

After the workspace question is addressed, the AFinchGUI script (appendix 2) runs and a GUI is displayed (fig. 9). The GUI accepts specifications for the hydrologic subregion and time period of interest, and controls and monitors AFINCH execution. A four-digit target hydrologic subregion (thsr) number is expected in the text box where the prompt "Number?" is displayed. A corresponding subdirectory "..\HSRthsr" is expected. The name of the hydrologic subregion may be entered in the field to the right of the hydrologic subregion number to facilitate identification. Standard names of hydrologic subregions are provided by Seaberand others (1987). The beginning and ending years specified by the user in the subsequent fields define the period of analysis (POA), from which the number of years in the analysis, *Ny*, is computed. The years of analysis are indexed by *iy* from 1 to *Ny*. Similarly, the month of analysis is indexed for each water year by *im* from 1 to 12, where the first month is October and the twelfth month is September.

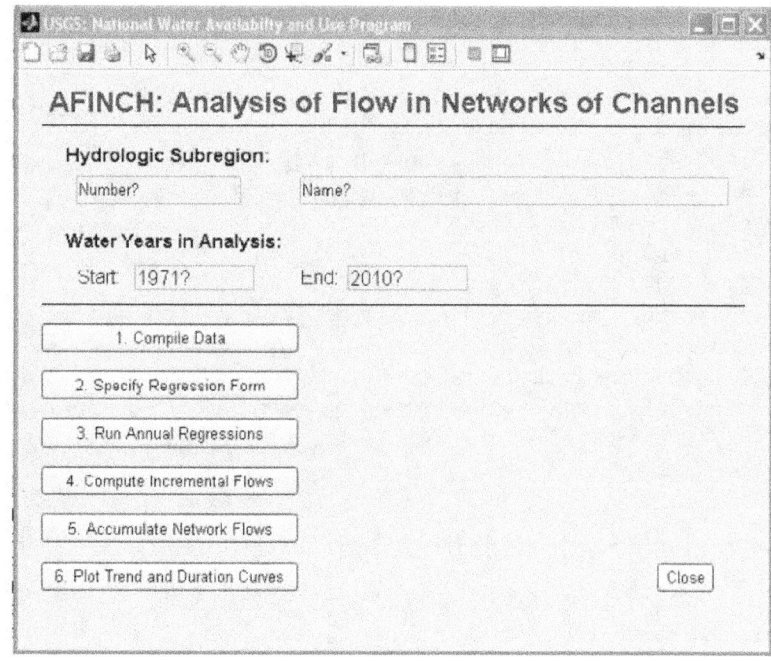

Figure 9. AFINCH graphical user interface to specify the hydrologic subregion and time period of interest and control program execution.

The Matlab scripts and functions executed through the GUI are listed in table 1. Note that the seven labeled push buttons on the AFINCH GUI correspond to the seven functions shown in blue text in table 1. The seven functions are expected to be executed in sequence to properly initialize variables in the Matlab workspace that are used in subsequent functions; otherwise, an error may occur.

Function CompileData

The function CompileData is run from the main AFINCH GUI by selecting the push button "1. Compile Data." The CompileData function initializes variables through the script (AFIniAFS truct, appendix 3) in the Matlab workspace and runs the AFSetupData script (appendix 4) for each year in the period of analysis (table 1). For each year in the period of analysis, AFSetupData runs a sequence of eight scripts that read in NHDPlus flowlines and catchments, monthly streamflow data for streamgages, water-use information associated with flowlines, precipitation and temperature data, and NLCD data. Data structures and variables are initialized and populated. Textual results are listed to the Matlab command window and the AFINCH GUI is updated to display progress and provide summary information. Figures are generated to display results for each year of the analysis. The following paragraphs describe the nine scripts associated with the CompileData function.

Table 1.   Generic filenames for Matlab scripts and functions underlying the AFINCH application.

[The generic filenames listed in the table do include versioning information, which is generally appended to the end of the filename prefix by an underscore "v" followed by the version identifier. For example, the current filename for the generic M-file AFinchGUI is AFinchGui_vld.m. All the functions are shown in blue font and can be initiated by clicking on buttons within the main AFINCH GUI. **Abbreviations:** Ny is the number of years in the analysis as determined from the specific beginning and ending water year; Nr is the number of explanatory variables specified in the regression]

Generic name of Matlab script or function	Appendix
AFinch	1
AFinchGU	2
CompileData	2 step 1
AFIniAFStruct	3
For $iy = 1$ to Ny	–
AFSetupData	4
AFReadNLCD	5
AFReadPrismPrec	6
AFGenStrucData	7
AFReadInFlowWY	8
AFStaBasinGridComIDWY	9
AFPlotAreasFlows	10
AFYieldImage	11
AFReadPrismTemp	12
End iy	–
AFGenLag1Precp	13
SpecifyRegression	2 step 2
AFBoxPlotExplanVar	14
For $ir = 1$ to Nr	–
AFCallRegCheckBox	15
AFRegCheckBoxGUI	16
End ir	–
AFRegressPOA	17
RunRegression	2 step 3
For $iy = 1$ to Ny	–
AFRegressByWY	18
End iy	–
AFPlotRegressCoeff	19
ComputeFlows	2 step 4
For $iy = 1$ to Ny	–
AFQEstAdjInc	20
AFQConAdjInc	21
AFPlotQmMeaEst	22
AFWrtQYEstCon	23
End iy	–
AccumulateFlows	2 step 5
For $iy = 1$ to Ny	–
AFConFlowAccum	24
End iy	–
PlotTrendDurations	2 step 6
AFTrendDurations	25
AFKenSen	26
PlotYieldsAtGages	2 step 7
AFYieldAtGagesGUI	27
AFImagePOAYield	28
AFid	29

Script AFReadNLCD

The script AFReadNLCD (appendix 5) reads catchment-based NLCD data and nhdflowline data for the target hydrologic region into the Matlab workspace. Flowline attributes include the *ComID*, the flowline length in kilometers, *LengthKm*, and the *ReachCode*. Because not all flowlines are associated with catchments, the difference between the number of flowlines and catchments is calculated and displayed for the user's information.

The first four digits of the *ReachCode* designate the hydrologic subregion. An indicator variable formed by comparing the first four digits of the *ReachCode* with the target hydrologic subregion is used to extract the hydrologic subregion data from the hydrologic region data. NLCD data similarly are restricted to the specified subregion.

Script AFReadPrismPrec

The Matlab script AFReadPrismPrec (appendix 6) inputs catchment gridcodes, drainage areas, and corresponding monthly PRISM precipitation data for the hydrologic region. The precipitation data for the specified hydrologic subregion is extracted, matched with the NLCD data, and stored in the Matlab workspace.

Script AFGenStrucData

The Matlab script AFGenStrucData (appendix 7) creates a Matlab variable to identify the catchments, with associated drainage areas, and flowlines on or upstream from streamgages operated in the processed water year. One text file is generated with ArcMap for each streamgage.

Script AFReadInFlowWY

The Matlab script AFReadInFlowWY (appendix 8) reads streamflow data for a set of historically operated streamgages, $\{S\}$, in the target hydrologic subregion that were active in the ith year, $\{s_{iy} \subset S\}$. Within each year of analysis, active streamgages are indexed by the variable *is* from 1 to the number of active streamgages in the iy^{th} year $\left|s_{iy}\right|$, which is represented by the variable Ns_{iy}. The monthly flow data populate a matrix $Q_s(iy, im)$ in which the stations are entered in downstream order. In addition, the set of drainage areas $\{A_s\}$ and flowlines $\{ComID_s\}$ corresponding to the historically operated streamgages are stored in the Matlab workspace.

In this report, $\subseteq ComID_{is}$ refers to the subset of all flowlines on or upstream from the flowline where the streamgage indexed by *is* in the iy^{th} year occurs. In addition, the script is used to identify flowlines where monthly water use has been documented and which are represented as the set $ComID_{WU}$ with corresponding monthly water-use values of $WU_{ComID}(iy, im)$. For each streamgage, the flowlines identified as the intersection of $\subseteq ComID_{is}$ with all flowlines where water use is specified, $ComID_{WU}$, are used to compute adjusted (natural) monthly flows as $Q'_s(iy, im) = Q_s(iy, im) - \sum WU_{\cap ComID_s}(iy, im)$. Negative water-use values are interpreted as water withdrawals, which imply that adjusted (natural) monthly flows would have been greater than measured flows. Similarly, positive water-use values are interpreted as streamflow augmentations, which imply that natural flows would have been less than the measured flows.

Script AFStaBasinGridComIDWY

The Matlab script AFStaBasinGridComIDWY (appendix 9) determines the catchments that are upstream from a streamgage but downstream from all upstream streamgages. In basins where the flow is monitored by more than one streamgage, catchments monitored by upstream streamgages are removed from the list of catchments monitored by downstream streamgages. In the process of removing these catchments, the network design matrix, N_{iy}, for each water year is developed.

The network design matrix is a lower triangular matrix of zeros and ones, which has dimension equal to the number of streamgages operated in the corresponding water year. Streamgages are represented by rows and columns in the matrix with streamgages in downstream order. Downstream order implies that streamgage numbers increase from top to bottom along the rows, *i*, and from left to right along the columns, *j*. The network design matrix is graded along its rows up to the diagonal, implying that element $a_{i,j} \le a_{i,j+1}$ for $i \le j$. A sample network design matrix is shown in figure 10. For example, two tributaries of the St. Joseph River are monitored upstream from streamgage 04097500 St. Joseph River at Three Rivers, MI: (1) 04096405 St. Joseph River at Burlington, MI, and (2) 04096515 South Branch Hog Creek near Allen, MI. Streamgages 04096405 and 04096515 do not drain any common areas.

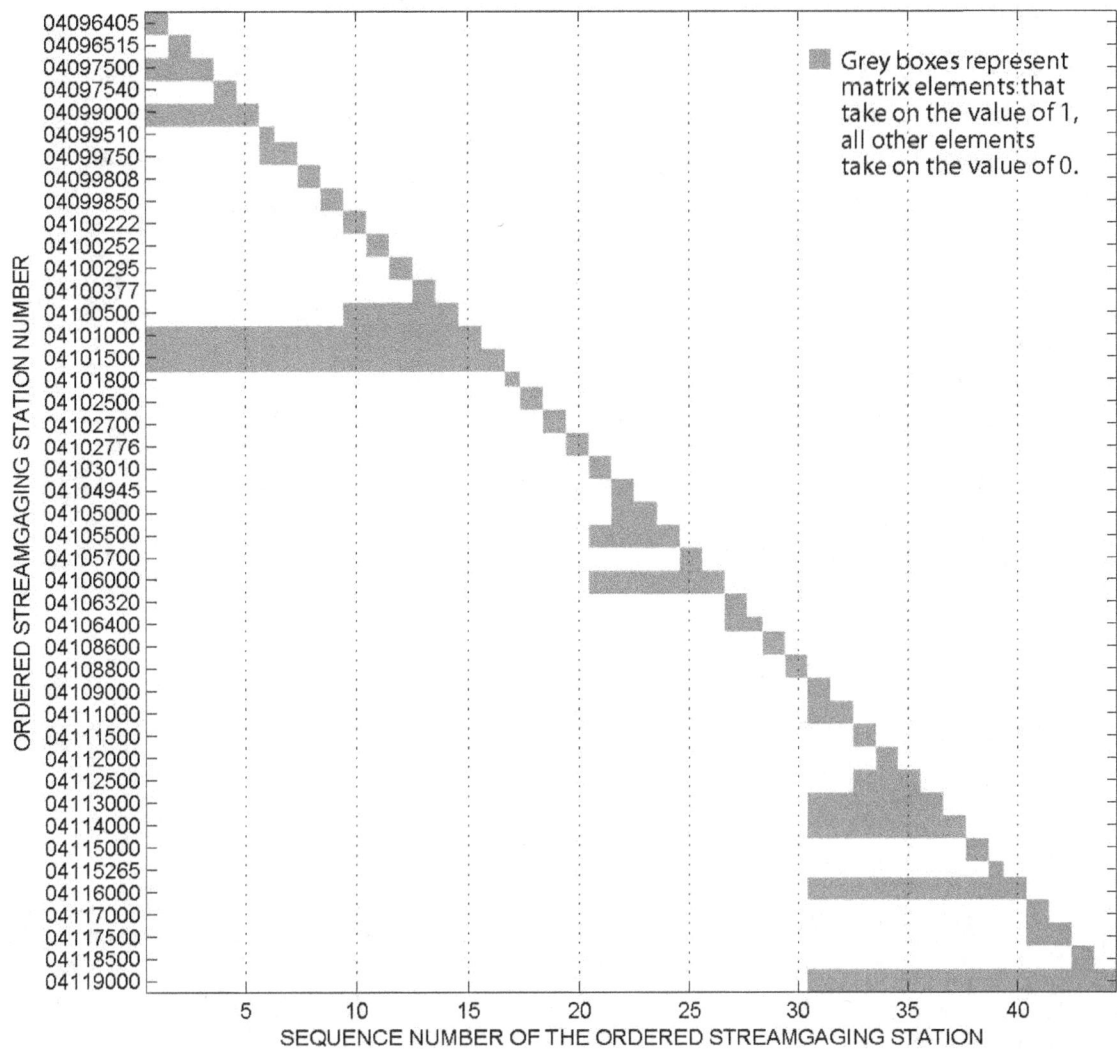

Figure 10. Streamgage network design matrix in water year 2000.

For all streamgages, incremental drainage areas (and incremental flows) are defined as drainage areas (and flows) in which drainage areas (and flows) monitored at any upstream streamgages have been subtracted. If no streamgages exist upstream from a particular streamgage, the total drainage area (and total flow) at that streamgage is equal to the incremental area (and flow). Incremental drainage areas (and flows) are computed by premultiplying the column vector of drainage areas (and measured flows) by the inverse of the network design matrix as $\Delta A_{s_{ty}} = N_{s_{ty}}^{-1} \cdot A_{s_{ty}}$. Notationally, the measured increment flows are represented as $\Delta Q'_{s_{ty}} = N_{s_{ty}}^{-1} \cdot Q_{s_{ty}}$, and incremental flows adjusted for water use are represented as $\Delta Q'_{s_{ty}} = N_{s_{ty}}^{-1} \cdot Q'_{s_{ty}}$. A list of streamgages monitored during a specific water year are listed to the computer screen during processing, along with their sequence number for the year under analysis and their sequence number for historically gaged basins.

Script AFPlotAreasFlows

The script AFPlotAreasFlows (appendix 10) plots the square root[3] of incremental NHDPlus drainage areas, determined by summing drainage areas of NHDPlus catchments uniquely monitored by a streamgage, against the square root of incremental NWIS drainage areas at streamgages (fig. 11). Small differences in the two measurements of drainage areas sometimes occur because of differences in drainage-area measurement methodologies. The plot provides an opportunity to detect large discrepancies, which may indicate an error in the catchment identification process. The script also plots the square root of incremental NHDPlus areas against the square root of incremental flows at streamgages by month (fig. 12).

Script AFYieldImage

The script AFYieldImage (appendix 11) creates an image showing the apparent incremental water yields at each gaging station, ΔY_s, by month for measured flows and a comparable image showing adjusted (natural) incremental water yields. Apparent water yields are computed as $\Delta Y_{s_{iy}} = \Delta Q_{s_{iy}} \div \Delta A_{s_{iy}}$, where the division operator indicates elementwise division, in which corresponding elements are divided, rather than matrix inversion and multiplication. Similarly, $\Delta Y' = \Delta Q'_{s_{iy}} \div \Delta A_{s_{iy}}$ indicates the adjusted (natural) incremental water yields, in which flows at streamgages have been adjusted for documented upstream water uses. The plots are intended to help the analyst identify anomalies in apparent water yields that may be resolved by water-use data. For example, water yields are expected to be positive (tinted blue) in hydrologic subregion 0405 for all months, with higher water yields during periods of relatively high precipitation and low evaporation, such as April. In Michigan, negative incremental water yields (tinted red) would not be expected under natural flow conditions.

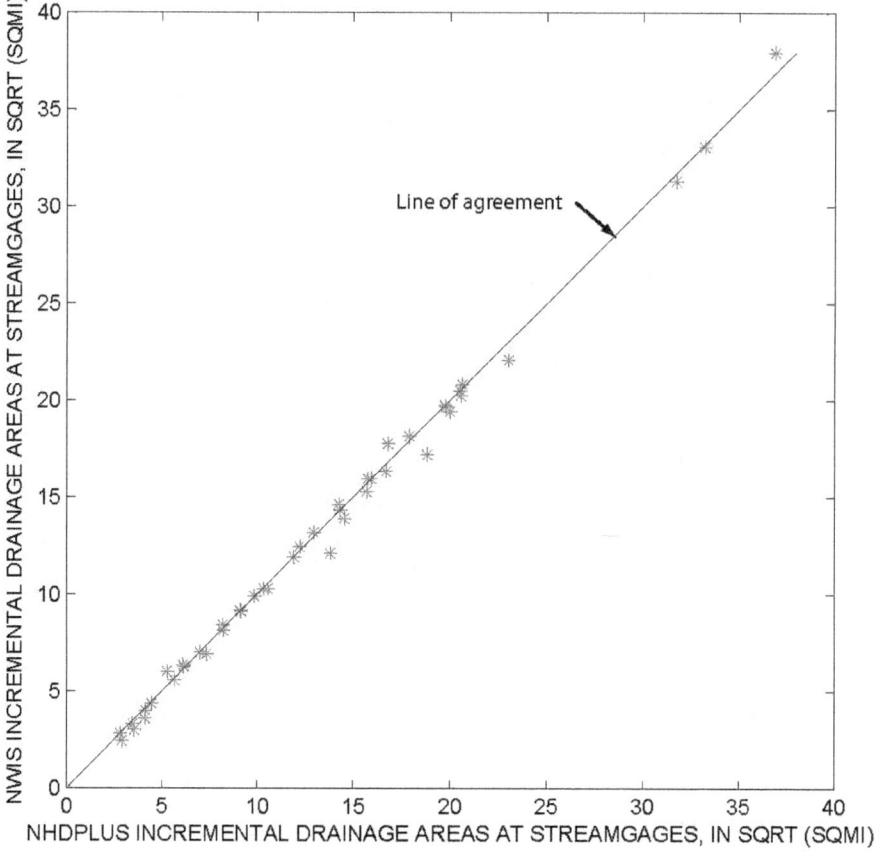

Figure 11.   Relation between the square root of incremental drainage areas indicated by the NHDPlus system and the square root of incremental drainage areas indicated by the U.S. Geological Survey National Water Information System at streamgaging stations for water year 2000. (SQRT, square root; SQMI, square mile; NWIS, National Water Information System)

Figure 13 shows monthly incremental water yields for water year 2000 for active streamgages in hydrologic subregion 0405. In this plot, streamgage 04106320 West Fork Portage Creek near Ostemo, MI (drainage area 13.0 mi[2]), and downstream streamgage 04106400 West Fork Portage Creek at Kalamazoo, MI (drainage area 18.7 mi[2]) have the lowest ranks of incremental water yields among active streamgages. This feature is readily apparent from the limited tint for all months in the two horizontal bands corresponding to these stations. Blumer and others (2001) remark that flow at these two stations is affected by ground-water withdrawals.

---

[3]The square-root transform was applied to reduce the positive (right) skewness that affects the distribution of drainage areas and flows. The transformed drainage areas (flows) are more uniformly distributed along the plots than the origninal metrics.

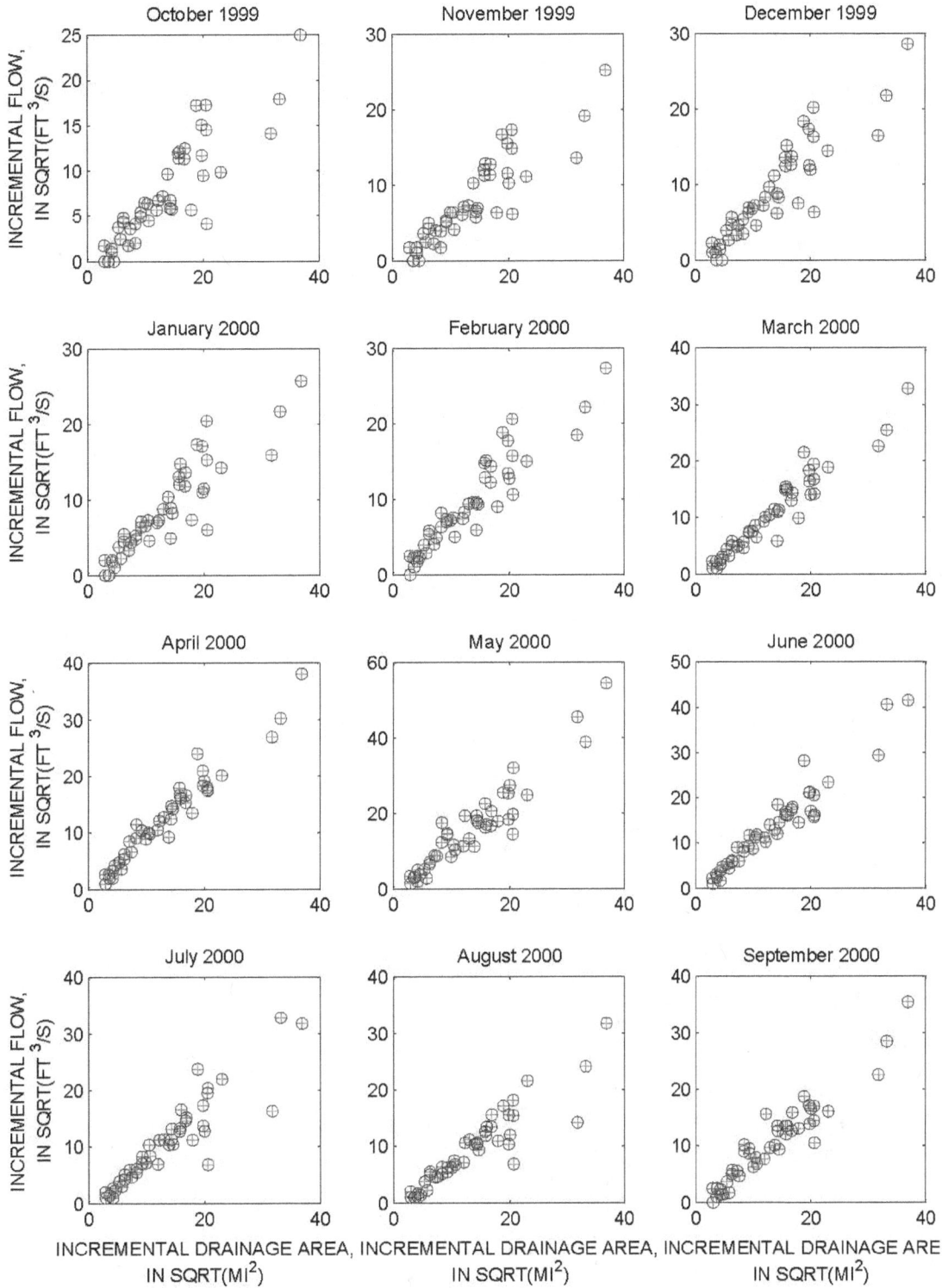

Figure 12.   Relation between the square root of incremental NHDPlus drainage areas and the square root of incremental flows at streamgages in hydrologic subregion 0405 by month. (SQRT, square root; FT³/s, cubic foot per second; MI², square mile)

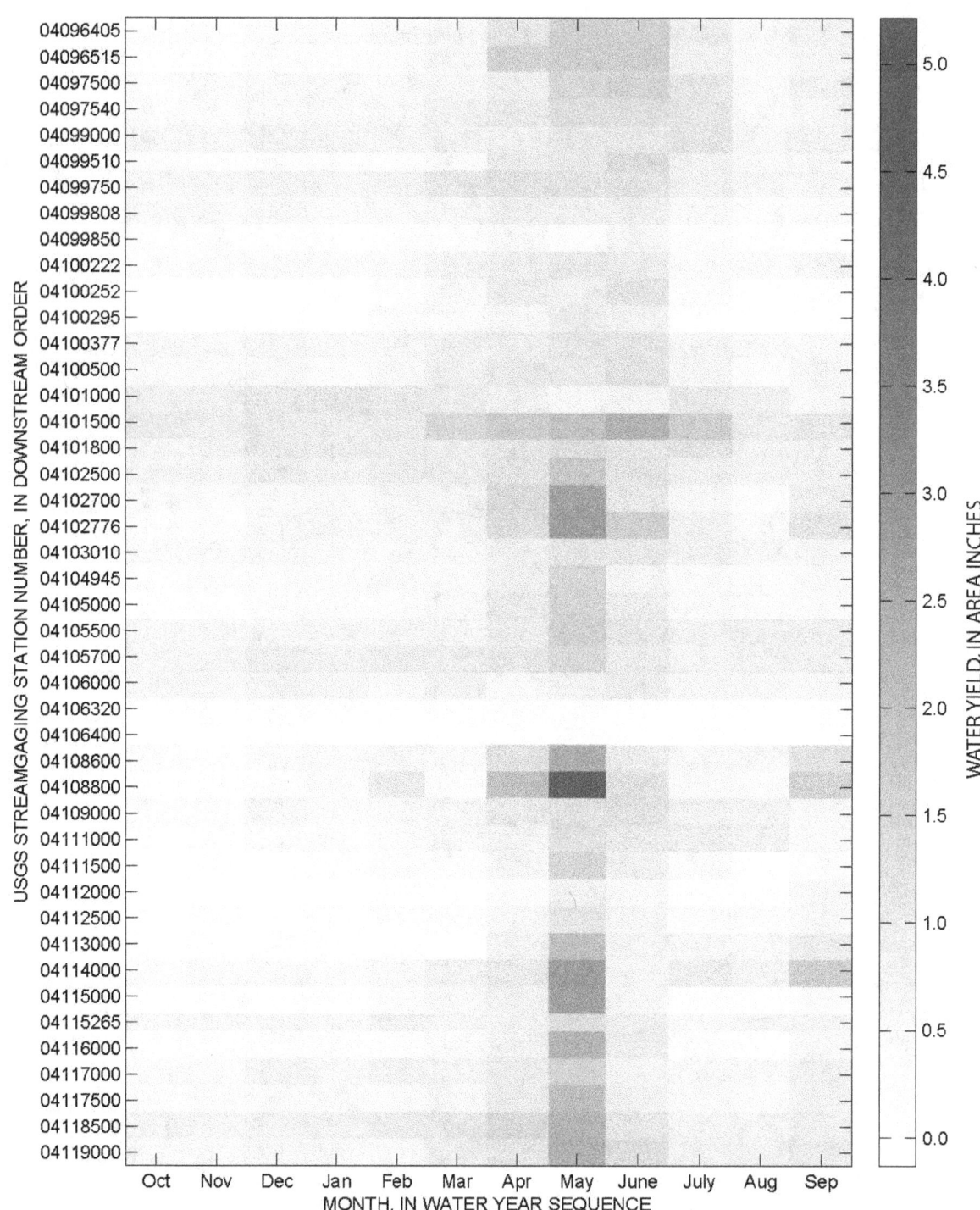

Figure 13.   Apparent incremental water yield at streamgages in 2000 within hydrologic subregion 0405.

Script AFReadPrismTemp

The script AFReadPrismTemp ([appendix 12](#)) inputs climatic data derived from data published by the PRISM Group. The data include the average of the monthly minimum and maximum air temperatures for each catchment in the subregion. Area-weighted climatic and land-cover data then are computed for incremental areas corresponding to incremental measured flows.

Script AFGenLag1Precp

The script AFGenLag1Precp ([appendix 13](#)) generates an array of lagged monthly precipitation values for each catchment in the specified period of record for the target hydrologic subregion. In particular, the array PrsmPremTHS is formed with the same dimension and shifted contents as PrsmPrecTHS. Thus, elements in PrsmPremTHS (year, catchment, month) correspond to elements in PrsmPrecTHS (year, catchment, month-1). The last month of the previous water year (September) is used for the first month (October) of the current water year. For example, for a specified period of record beginning in October 2000 (the first month of water year 2001), the monthly flow for September 2000 (the last month of water year 2000) is used.

Function SpecifyRegression

The function SpecifyRegression is run from the main AFINCH GUI by selecting the push button "2. Specify Regression Form." The function displays an input dialog box for the user to specify the number of candidate explanatory variables, *Nr*, in the multiple regression models for estimating monthly water yields. Then, scripts are initiated to facilitate the display and selection of explanatory variables.

The general form of the multiple regression equation for estimating water yield is

$$\Delta Y'_{s_{iy,im}} = \sum_{ir=0}^{Nr(im)} X_{s_{iy,ir(im)}} \cdot \hat{\beta}_{ir(im)} + \varepsilon_{iy,im} ,\qquad (1)$$

where

$\Delta Y'_{s_{iy,im}}$ is the vector of incremental monthly water yields for the period of analysis at streamgages adjusted for water use;

$X_{s_{iy,ir(im)}}$ is the regression design matrix, which includes the user-specified, candidate explanatory variables in the monthly regression equations augmented by a leading column of ones. The number of columns in X can vary by month;

$\hat{\beta}_{ir(im)}$ is a vector of parameter estimates associated with the monthly explanatory variables, where the vector length can vary by month; and

$\varepsilon_{iy,im}$ is the vector of monthly regression residuals (error components).

The index for *ir* starts at 0 rather than one to indicate that constants are included in the monthly regression equations.

Script AFBoxplotExplanVar

Once the maximum number of regression variables, *Nr*, is specified, the monthly distribution of precipitation ([fig. 14](#)) and temperature data ([fig. 15](#)), and the annual distribution of the percentage of areas of each NLCD code ([fig. 16](#)) are displayed as boxplots by the script AFBoxplotExplanVar ([appendix 14](#)). The boxplots are intended as an aid to the selection of explanatory variables for the regression analysis. For example, the percentage of areas for some NLCD codes are zero for all catchments in a hydrologic subregion. The distributions of percentage of areas for these NLCD codes are displayed as horizontal red lines at zero on the y-axis and would be inappropriate choices for explanatory variables because they would not increase the column space (explanatory potential) of the regression design matrix.

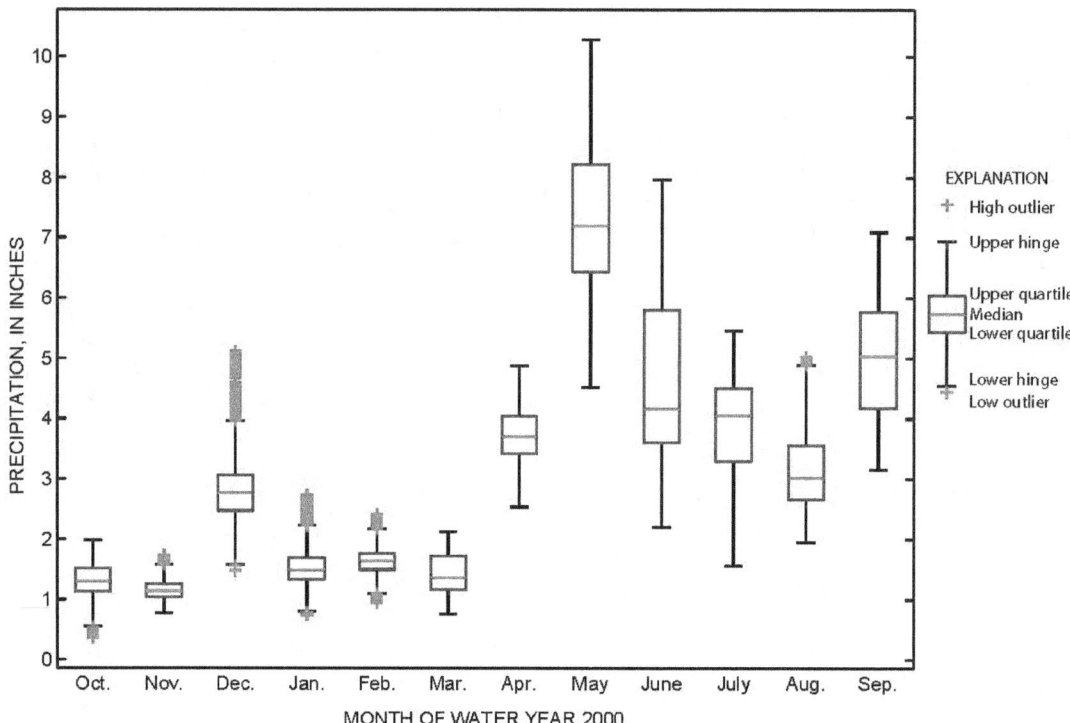

Figure 14. Distribution of monthly precipitation among basins with U.S. Geological Survey streamgages in water year 2000 for hydrologic subregion 0405.

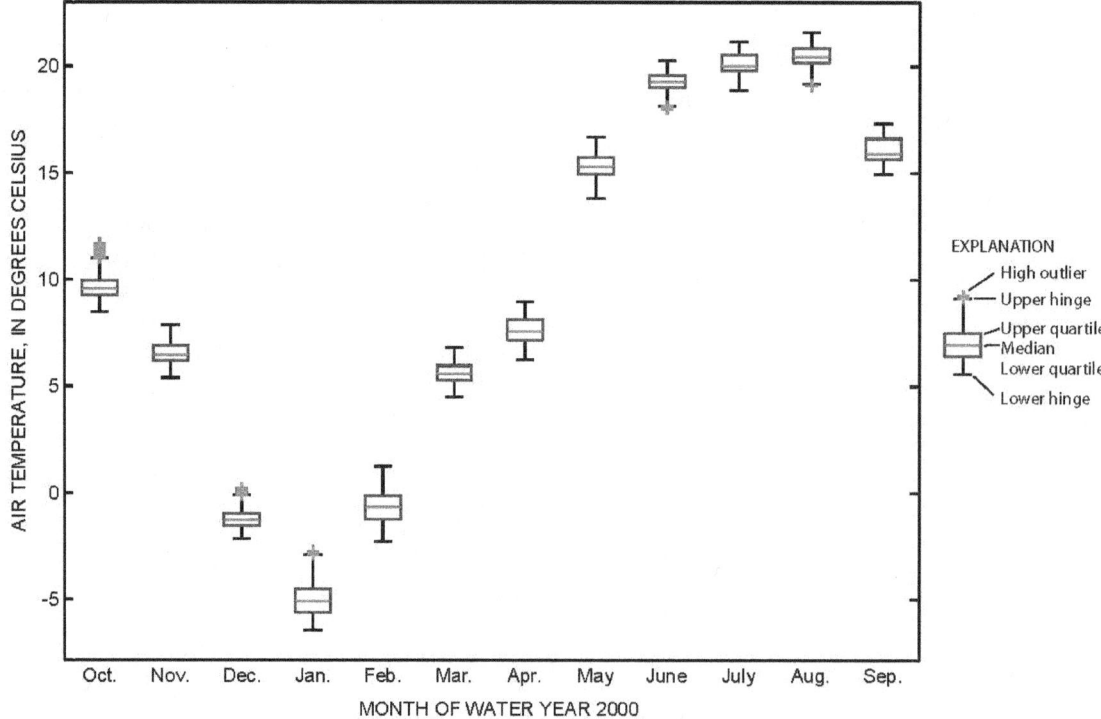

Figure 15. Distribution of monthly air temperatures in water year 2000 among catchments in hydrologic subregion 0405.

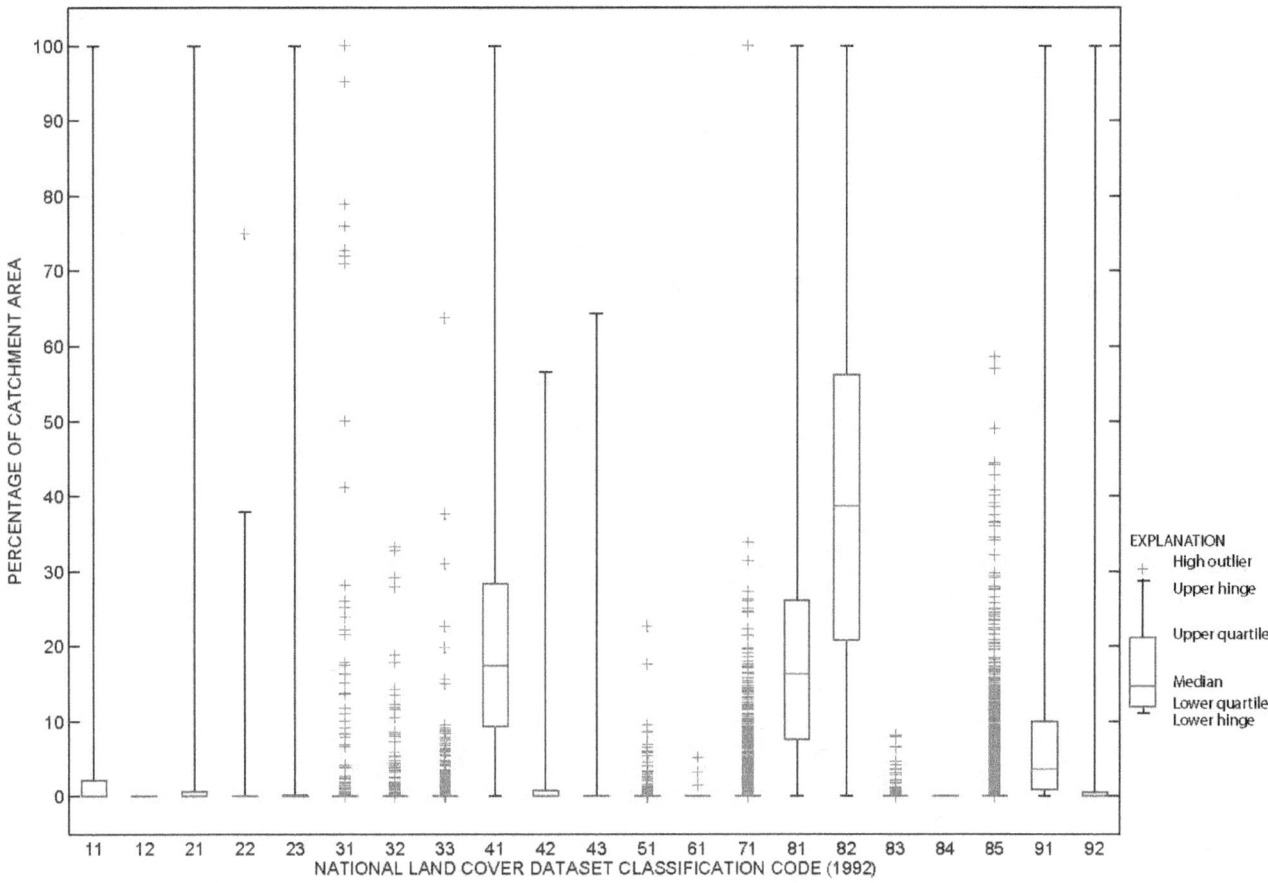

Figure 16.   Distribution of percentage of areas among National Land Cover Characteristic codes for catchments in hydrologic subregion 0405.

Script AFCallRegCheckBox

The script AFCallRegCheckBox (appendix 15) initializes a default name for each explanatory variable and runs the script AFRegCheckBoxGUI (appendix 16). The GUI provides an interface for selecting the explanatory variables or variable components in the regression equation. Variables or components are selected by checking one or more boxes next to the NLCD variable codes, or next to the climatic variables of precipitation or temperature (fig. 17). Once the desired check boxes are selected, the user may specify a variable name or accept the default name based on the sequence number of the regression variable from 1 to *Nr*. If checks are placed before multiple land-use classes, the total percentage of the area for all selected classes is computed as

the regression variable. For example, if checks were placed in front of 51 Shrubland and 71 Grasslands/Herbaceous (fig. 17), a gaged area having 2 percent of the land area classified as 51 Shrubland and 3 percent as 71 Grasslands/Herbaceous would return a value of 5 for the variable at that gaged area. Multiple explanatory variables can be formed from different combinations of NLCD variable codes.

After the Submit button (fig. 17) is pressed, the selected variable is added to the regression set, and a boxplot showing the distribution of selected variables among catchments is displayed (fig. 18). The boxplots show the distributions of each selected variable. The GUI for forming regression variables and boxplots for displaying variable distributions will be redisplayed until all *Nr* variables are specified.

Script AFRegressPOA

The script AFRegressPOA (appendix 17) facilitates development of a multiple regression equation for each month of the water year based on monthly data for the entire period of analysis (POA). A stepwise variable selection process (The MathWorks, 2008b) is used to develop the equations using a subset of the variables specified as possible explanatory variables. The user is prompted for α-values[4] to determine variable entry and removal from the stepwise selection process. In stepwise regression, subsets of possible explanatory variables are iteratively evaluated. In each iteration, parameters associated with variables are estimated and their associated p-values[5] are computed. If the p-value of any estimated parameter is less than the specified α-value, the corresponding variable is added or retained. The variable with the largest p-value greater than the α-value is removed. The process continues until p-values for all included variables are less than the specified α-values.

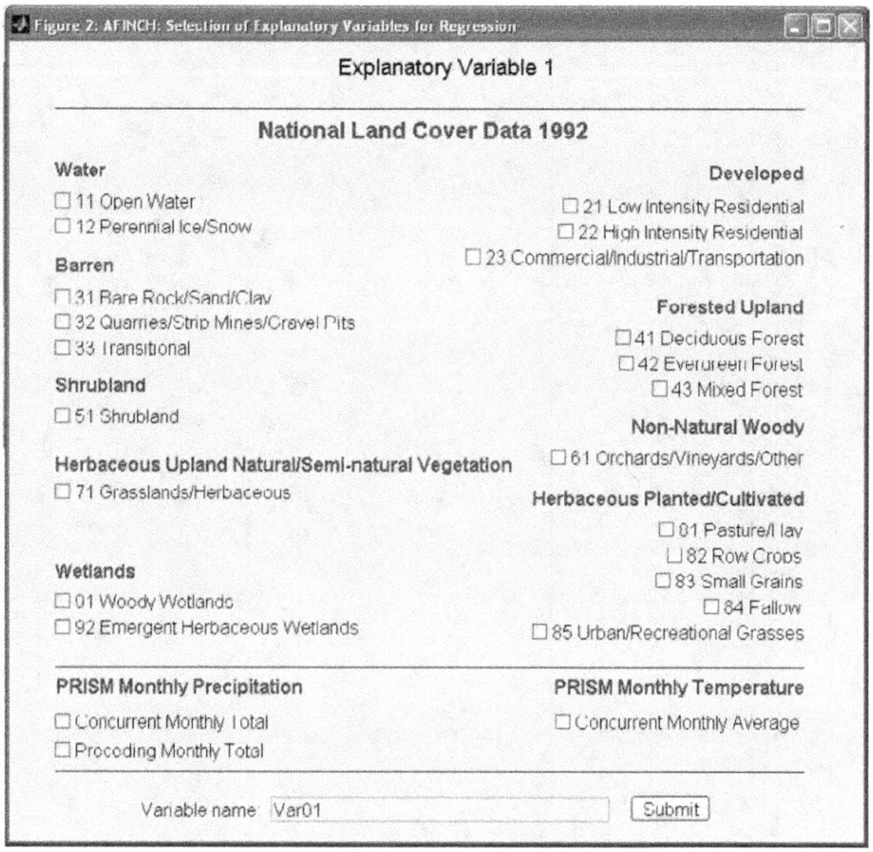

Once stepwise regressions are developed for each month, a plot of the results of the regression variable selection process for the period of record is displayed. The plot shows a grid of variables by month. For each month represented by a column of grid cells, variables (rows) with estimated parameters that are significantly greater than zero, based on the specified α-value, are filled with blue, those with estimated parameters significantly less than zero are filled with red, and variables that are not significant are filled with white. If desired, candidate variables for the regression can be respecified by selecting the push button "2. Specify Regression Form" (fig. 9), or annual regressions can be computed using the identified form for the period of record regression equation by selecting the push button "3. Run Annual Regressions."

Using data for the period 1971 to 2000 in hydrologic region 0405 and the candidate regression variables shown in figure 18 as an example, an image of the regression variable selection results is shown in figure 19. The image indicates

Figure 17. Graphical user interface for selecting explanatory variables for use in a multiple regression equation to estimate water yields.

that the parameters associated with both concurrent and preceding monthly precipitation variables were positively associated with water yields at a specified α-value of 0.002 or less for each month of the year. Significant parameters associated with the NLCD categorized as Developed (which includes class codes 21 and 22 for low- and high-intensity residential areas, respectively, and code 23 for commercial, industrial, and transportation land uses) were negative. This indicates a negative statistical association between water yield and Developed land in the 9 months from November through July, but no statistically significant relation in the months of August, September, and October, given the other variables in the regression equation. Concurrent monthly temperature was positively associated with water yield in January and February, but negatively associated with water yield in March, April, and May. Warmer temperatures in January and February may result in greater snow melt and consequent flows in the

---

[4]An α-value is a pre-specified probability for a Type 1 (or false positive) error. In the context of this report, the α-value expresses the risk, which an analyst is willing to accept, that a selected variable could be included in the regression equation when, in fact, the variable is not statistically associated to water yield.

[5]A p-value is the probability that the null hypothesis is true given the data. In regression analysis, the null hypothesis is generally that the estimated parameter associated with the corresponding explanatory variable is zero.

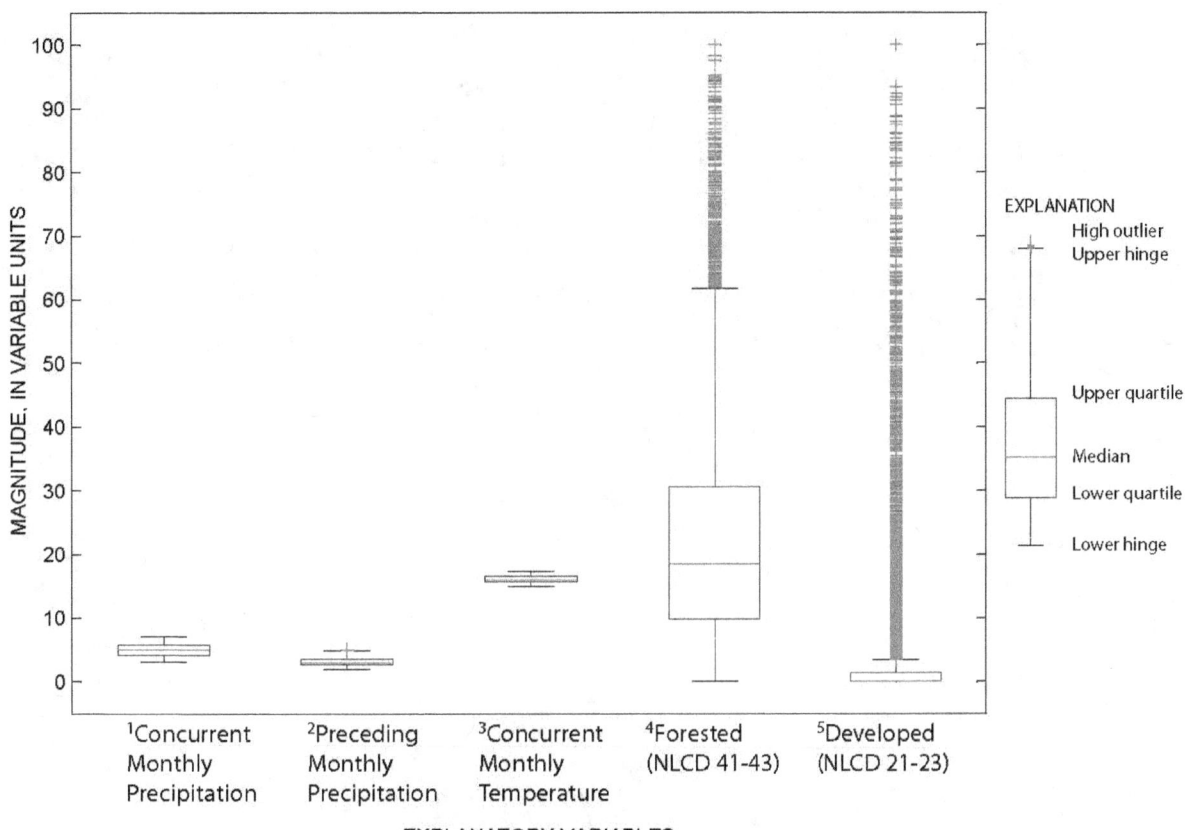

Figure 18. Distribution of selected regression variables among catchments in hydrologic subregion 0405 in September 2000.

[1] The distribution of precipitation values among catchments in hydrologic subregion 0405 during the last month of the specified period (September 2000), in inches. The monthly precipitation values are concurrent with the corresponding monthly water yields.

[2] The distribution of precipitation values among catchments in hydrologic subregion 0405 during the second to last month of the specified period (August 2000), in inches. Preceding monthly precipitation refers to precipitation in the month prior to the corresponding monthly water yields.

[3] The distribution of air temperature values among catchments in hydrologic subregion 0405 during the last month of the specified period (September 2000), in degrees Celsius.

[4] National Land Cover Data (NLCD) areas characterized as Forested include class codes 41—Deciduous Forest, 42—Evergreen Forests, and 43—Mixed Forest.

[5] National Land Cover Data (NLCD) areas characterized as Developed include class codes 21—Low Intensity Residential, 22—High Intensity Residential, and 23—Commercial/Industrial/Transportation.

first 2 months of the year. Assuming monthly temperatures are (positively) autocorrelated, the early snowmelt may have reduced water available in March, April, and May. Land characterized as Forested (which includes NLCD class code 41 for Deciduous Forest, code 42 for Evergreen Forest, and code 43 for Mixed Forest) was positively associated with water yield in the months from July through November,

negatively associated with water yield in March and April, and not statistically associated with water yield in the remaining months. A statistical association identified in regression analysis does not necessarily imply that a causal relation exists between the corresponding explanatory and response variables. Table 2 shows summary statistics for the monthly regression equations.

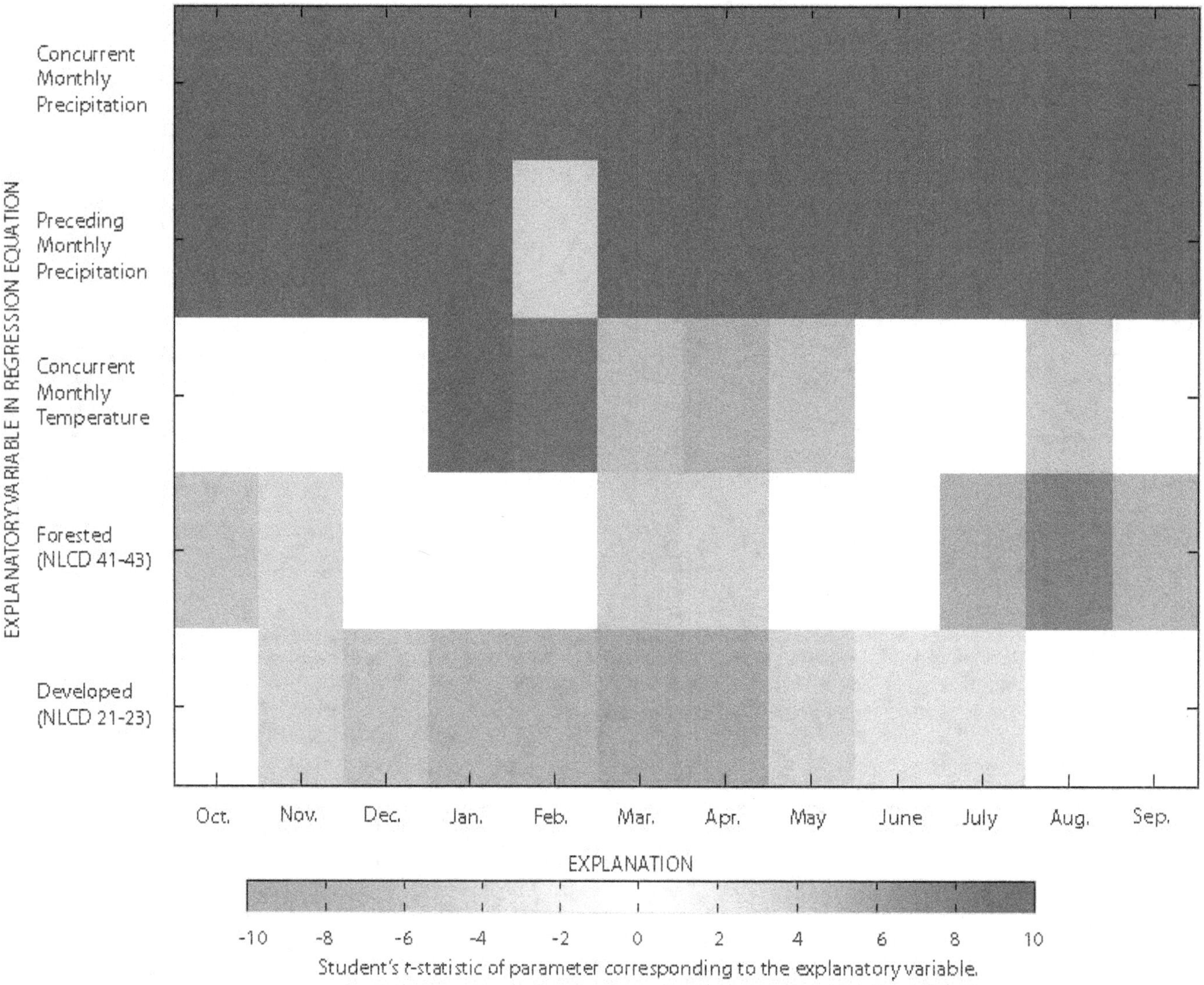

Figure 19.   Significant monthly regression parameters associated with specified variables developed for water years 1971 to 2000 by the use of data from hydrologic subregion 0405. (Value of the Student's *t*-statistic associated with the probability that the true value of the parameter for the corresponding explanatory variable equals zero, given the data. The sign of the *t*-statistic is consistent with the sign of the corresponding parameter. A *t*-statistic with an absolute value greater than 2 is commonly interpreted as indicating statistical significance.)

Table 2. Summary statistics for monthly regression equations for estimating water yields using data for water years 1971 to 2000.

Month	Number of explanatory variables	Number of degrees of freedom	Root mean square error	F-statistics	p-value	Coefficient of determination
October	3	1,407	0.4625	263.21	<0.000001	0.3595
November	4	1,406	.4564	251.13	<0.000001	.4167
December	3	1,407	.4866	252.59	<0.000001	.3500
January	4	1,406	.5677	217.68	<0.000001	.3824
February	4	1,406	.5778	156.88	<0.000001	.3086
March	5	1,405	.7466	168.19	<0.000001	.3744
April	5	1,405	.5950	87.92	<0.000001	.2383
May	4	1,406	.5011	191.60	<0.000001	.3528
June	3	1,407	.5411	307.17	<0.000001	.3958
July	4	1,406	.4062	137.20	<0.000001	.2808
August	4	1,406	.3665	111.69	<0.000001	.2411
September	3	1,407	.4109	200.50	<0.000001	.2995

Function RunRegression

The function RunRegression is initiated from the main AFINCH GUI by selecting push button "3. Run Annual Regressions." The function RunRegression initiates scripts that compute monthly regression estimates of incremental water yield at streamgages for each water year based on explanatory variables in the period of analysis. In addition, the monthly regression parameters estimated by ordinary least-squares and robust regression are plotted with the monthly regression parameter estimate for the period of record.

Script AFRegressByWY

The script AFRegressByWY (appendix 18) is used to estimate annual regression parameters for computing incremental water yields by use of ordinary least-squares $\hat{\beta}$ and robust methods $\tilde{\beta}$ (The MathWorks, 2008b). Although the ordinary least-squares (OLS) estimates generally are less certain when standard regression assumptions (Stapleton, 1995) are met and have readily computed confidence limits, robust parameter estimates may be more indicative of the general relation between the explanatory variables if data anomalies are present, water uses are not fully accounted for, or standard assumptions are not fully met. Data anomalies may be caused by numerous factors, including undocumented water uses. The Pearson coefficient of determination, which characterizes the percentage of variability in water yields explained by regression, is computed for the robust regression results and displayed for each month as a measure of the model fit.

As an example of this application, figure 20 shows regression relations between adjusted incremental water yields, $\Delta Y'_{s_{(y,m)}}$, and estimated water yields,

$\Delta \hat{\tilde{Y}}'_{s_{(y,m)}} = \left(X_{s_{(y,ir(im))}} \cdot \tilde{B}_{iy\,ir(im)} \right)$, by month using the model form shown in figure 19. In the example, parameters were estimated on the basis of data for water year 1971 only. For the 30-year period from 1971 to 2000, the median monthly Pearson coefficients of determination between measured and estimated water yields varied from 0.1443 for May to 0.3924 for September (fig. 21).

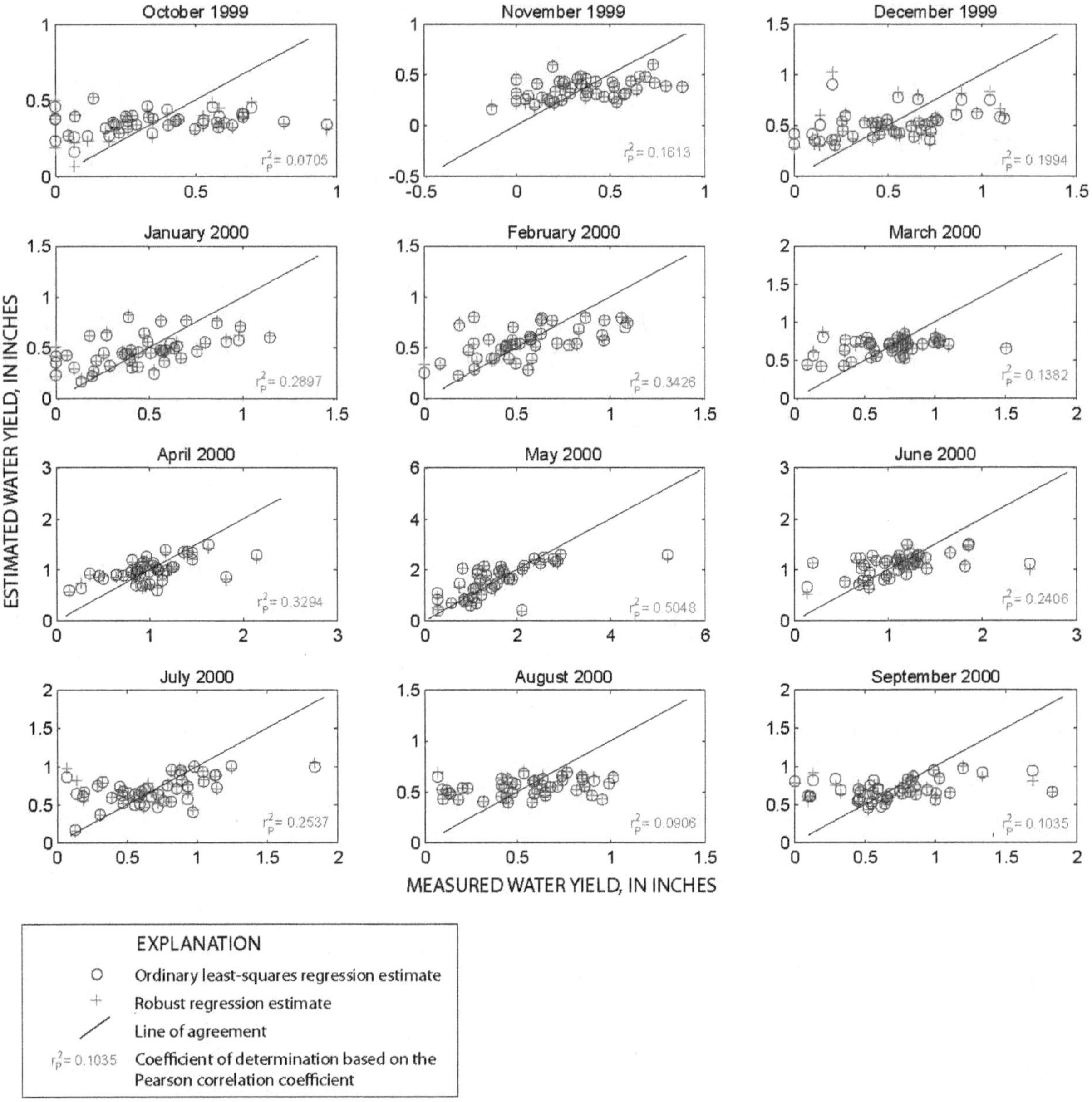

Figure 20.   Relation between the estimated and measured water yields by month for water year 2000 using regression model forms developed in the period-of-record analysis for hydrologic subregion 0405.

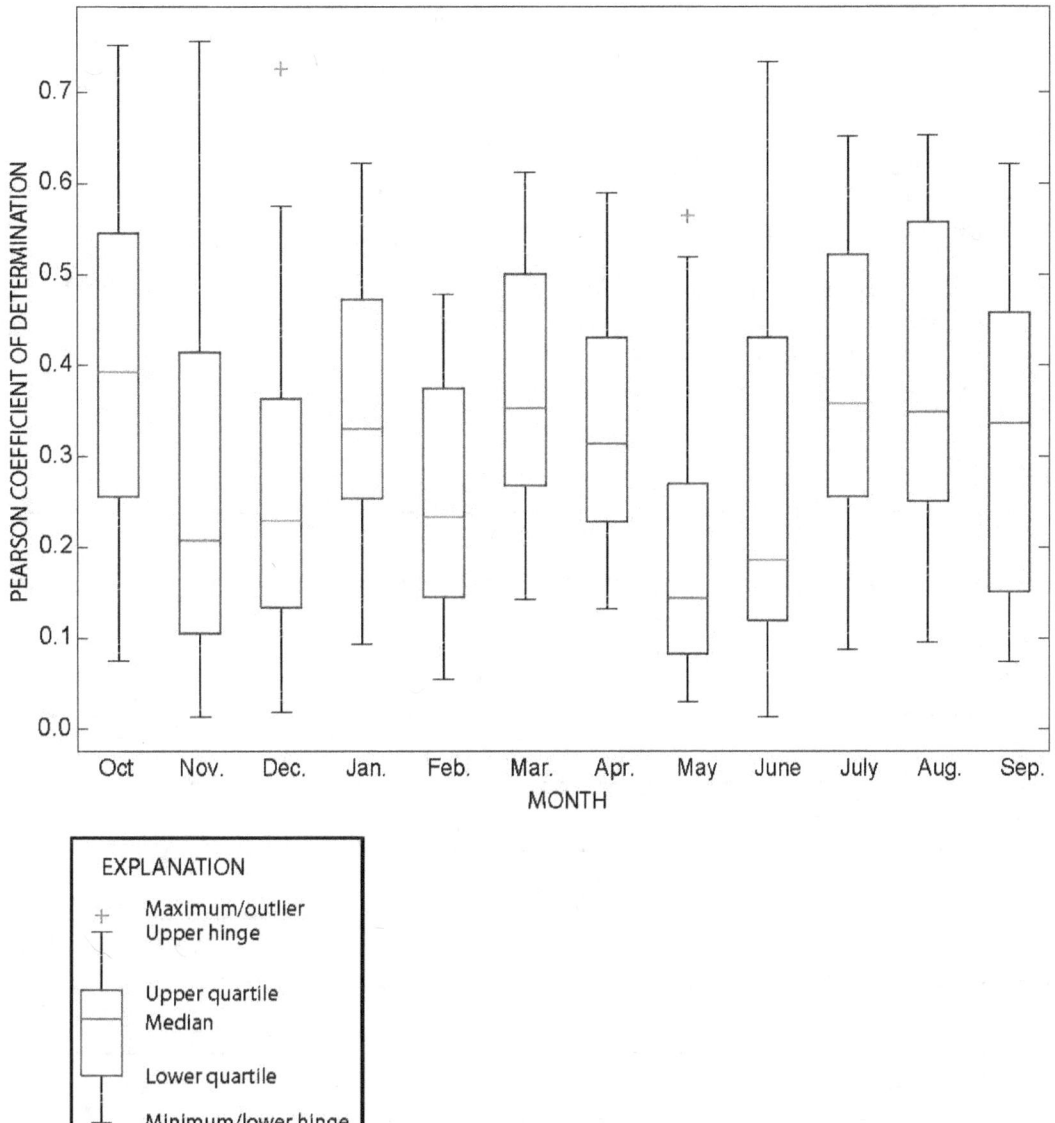

Figure 21. Distribution of Pearson coefficients of determination between measured and estimated monthly water yields for water years 1971 to 2000.

Script AFPlotRegressCoeff

The script AFPlotRegressCoeff ([appendix 19](#)) plots times series of annual regression coefficients for the period of analysis for each calendar month. Theses plots show the annual OLS parameter estimates, $\hat{\beta}_{iy,im(ir)}$ with blue 'o' and robust parameter estimates, $\hat{\beta}_{iy,im(ir)}$, with red '×'. All estimates are computed on the basis of explanatory variables selected based on monthly analysis of data from the entire period of analysis. The OLS parameter estimates are indicated with a blue vertical bar that depicts the 95-percent confidence interval about the estimate. A dashed line is plotted at zero on the y-axis for reference. The horizontal green line shows the OLS parameter estimate from the period-of-record analysis. For the example regression shown in [figure 19](#), a time series plot for October parameters is shown in [figure 22](#), and for June parameters is shown in [figure 23](#).

Function ComputeFlows

The function ComputeFlows is initiated from the main AFINCH GUI by selecting push button "4. Compute Incremental Flows." The function initiates the three scripts below.

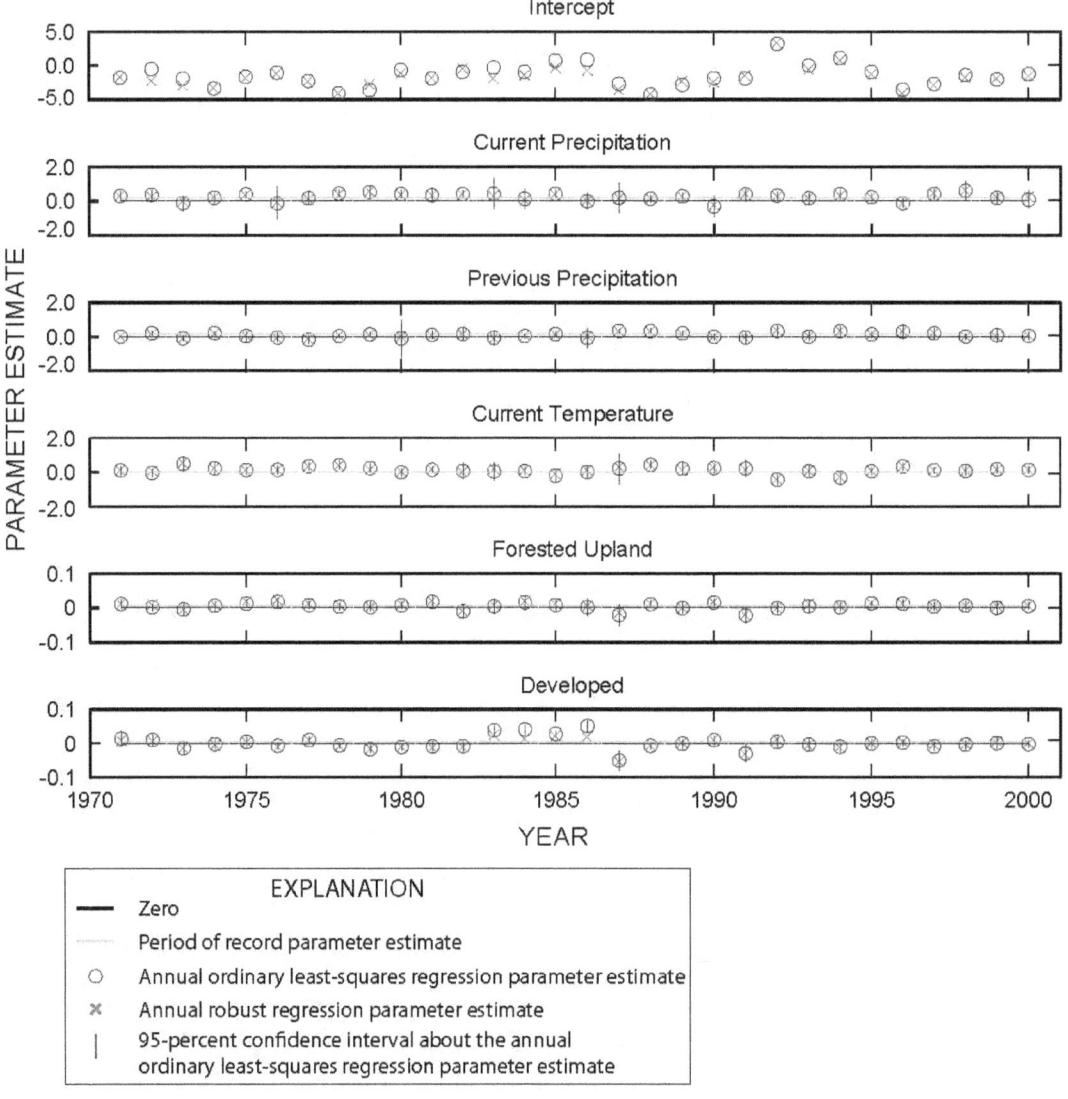

Figure 22. Regression parameters for estimating October water yield for water years 1971 to 2000.

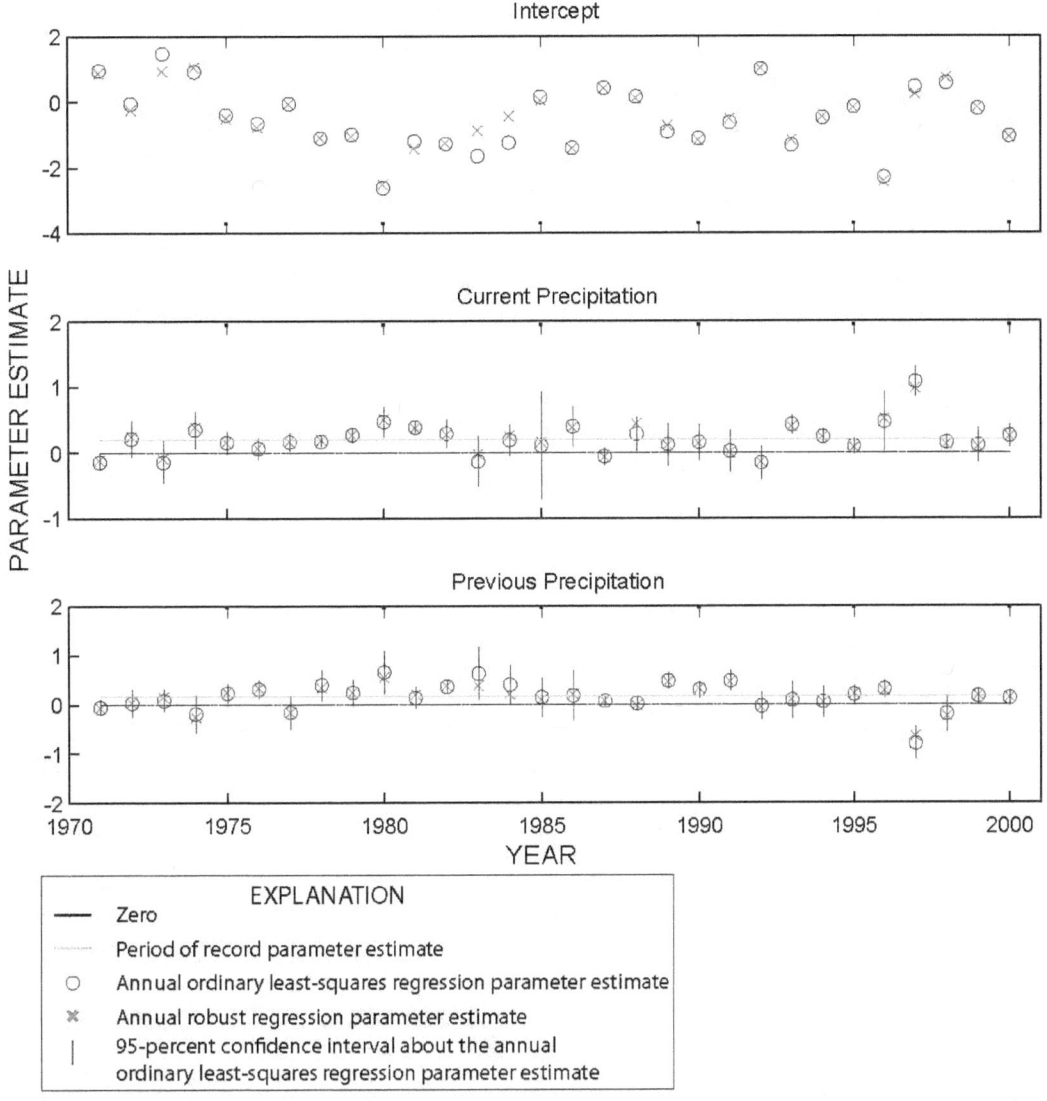

Figure 23. Regression parameters for estimating June water yield for water years 1971 to 2000.

Script AFQEstAdjInc

The script AFQEstAdjInc (appendix 20) computes estimates of water yield for all catchments on the basis of the period-of-record form of the monthly regression equations. Robust parameter estimates are determined and used to compute adjusted water-yield estimates, $\hat{\tilde{y}}'_{cat}$, that are specific to the month and water year of the analysis and consistent with specified water-use data. Water-yield estimates are reported in units of area inches. Corresponding flows from catchments, $\hat{\tilde{q}}'_{cat}$, to flowlines, $\hat{\tilde{q}}'_{Fl}$, are estimated by multiplying the estimated catchment yields by drainage areas and reported in cubic feet per second.

Script AFQConAdjInc

The script AFQConAdjInc (appendix 21) sums estimated flows from upstream flowlines (Fl) that are not monitored by upstream gages, $\cap Fl$, as $\Delta \hat{\tilde{Q}}_S = \sum_{\cap Fl} \hat{\tilde{q}}_{Fl}$ to estimate incremental flows from gaged basins. The ratio of the incremental measured flow to the incremental estimated flow, $\Delta Q_S / \Delta \hat{\tilde{Q}}_S$, is computed for each gaged basin for each month of the analysis. These ratios are multiplied by the estimated flows, $\hat{\tilde{q}}_{Fl}$, to constrain the resulting flows, $\check{\tilde{q}}_{Fl}$, so that the sum of these flows match incremental measured flows, $\Delta \check{\tilde{Q}}_S \equiv \Delta Q_S$. Corresponding constrained water yields, $\check{\tilde{y}}'_{cat}$, are computed for each catchment.

Script AFPlotQmMeaEst

The script AFPlotQmMeaEst ([appendix 22](#)) plots a matrix of estimated, $\Delta\hat{Q}_S$, and measured, ΔQ_S, monthly incremental flows for gaged basins for each year of the analysis. Flows were readjusted for any specified water use. Because the distributions of flow magnitudes generally are positively skewed (elongated tail at the right), a square-root transformation was applied to the plotted flows to improve the visualization. At some sites, the incremental flows are negative in some months and water years, which cannot be plotted following a square-root transformation. To complete the plot and the computation of correlation, negative flows are identified and removed from the plotted flows, and a message is displayed in the command window to notify the user of the omitted observations. The line of agreement is plotted and the Spearman coefficient of determination, which is based on the ranks of all non-negative paired flow values, is displayed on each plot to provide a measure of fit ([fig. 24](#)). The median Spearman coefficient of determination between measured and estimated incremental flows varied from 0.8846 for September to 0.9682 for May for the period from 1971 to 2000 ([fig. 25](#)).

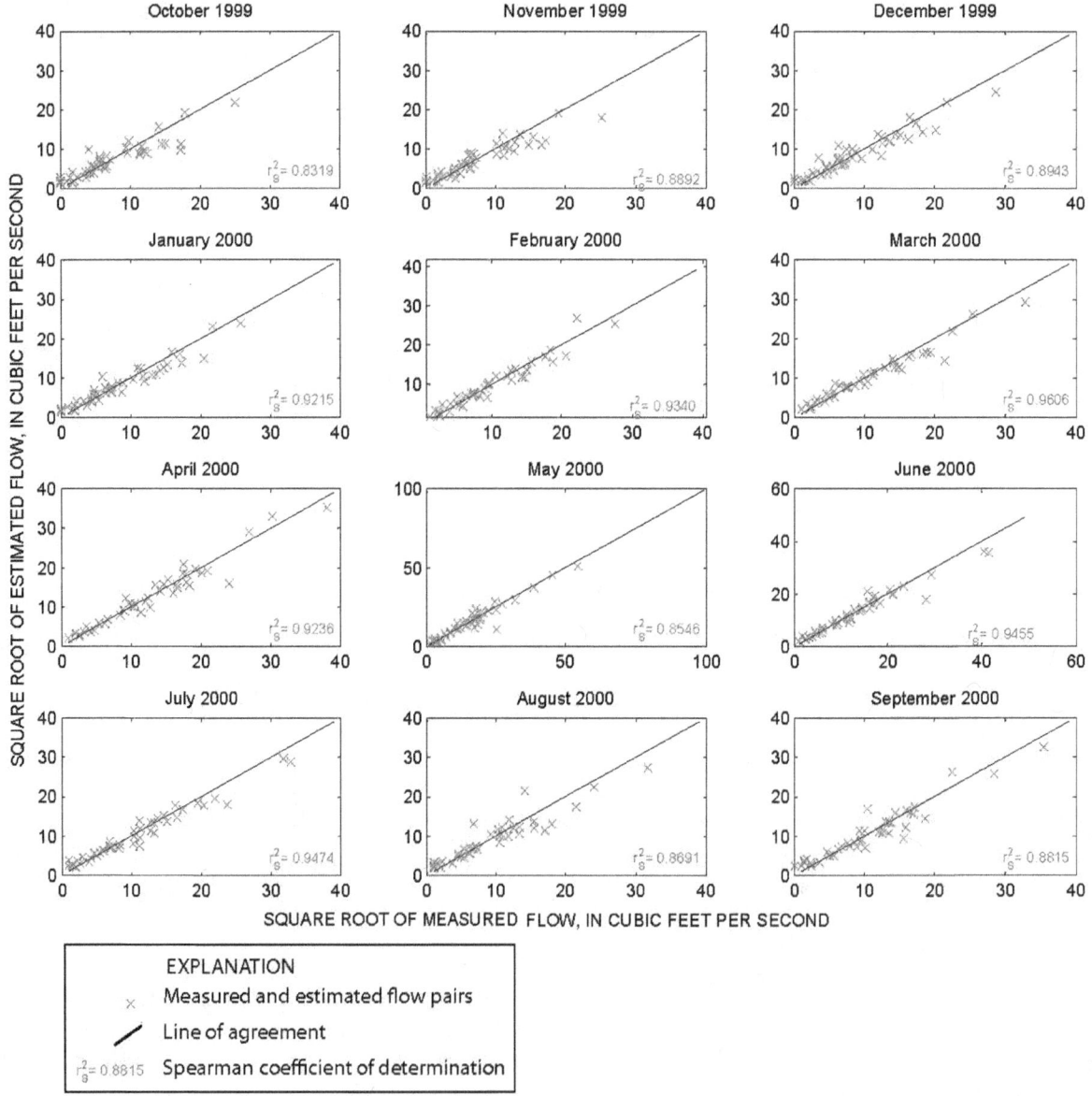

Figure 24. Measured and estimated incremental flows at gaged basins within hydrologic subregion 0405 in water year 2000 by month.

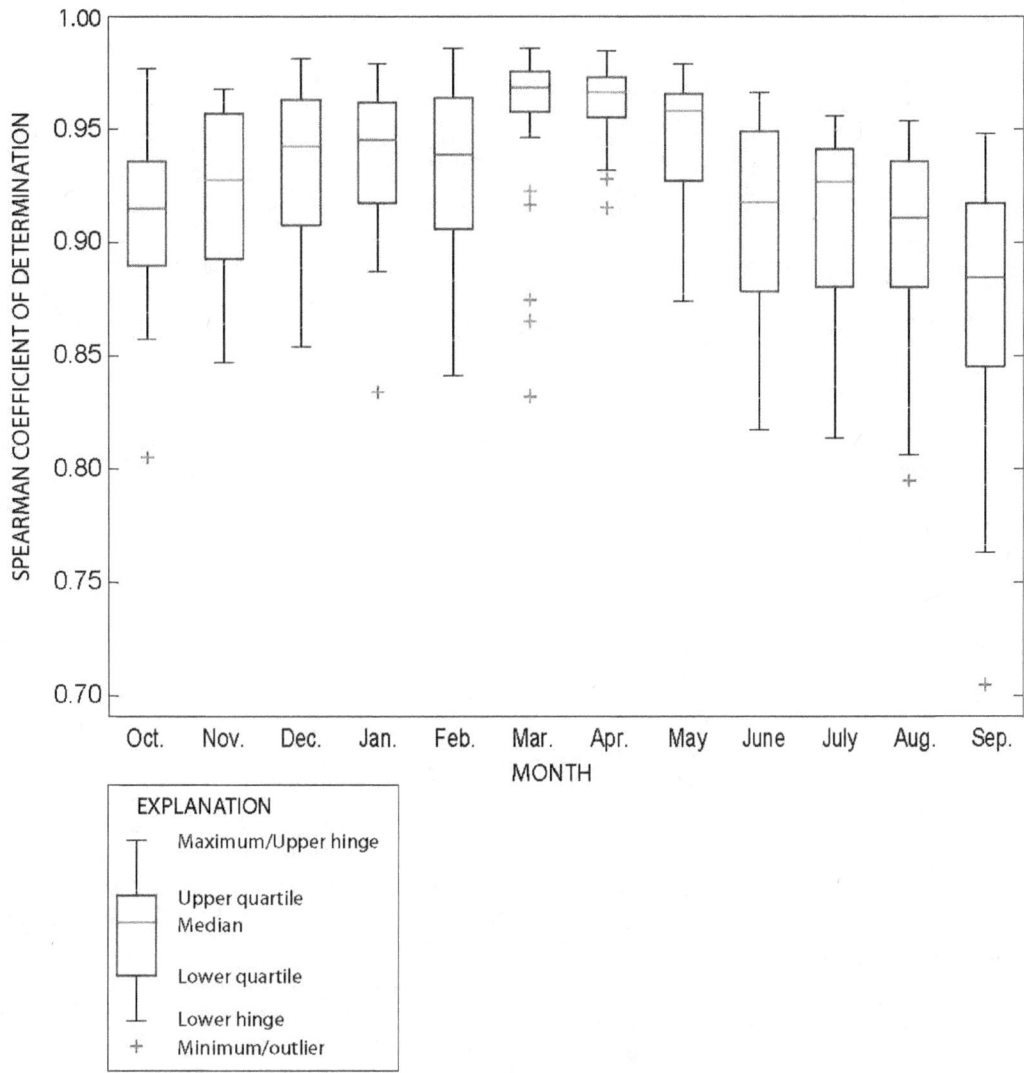

Figure 25. Monthly distribution of Spearman's coefficients of determination between measured and estimated incremental flows for water years 1971 to 2000.

Script AFWrtQYEstCon

The script AFWrtQYEstCon (appendix 23) writes monthly constrained and unconstrained estimates of flow at flowlines, in cubic feet per second, and water yield at catchments, in area inches, adjusted for water use, to a comma-delimited file for each year of the analysis. A header line is output with field names as the first line in each file. Each subsequent line of each output file contains information for one catchment in the hydrologic subregion. The output fields include *Grid_Code*, *ComID*, *AreaSqMi* (catchment area in square miles), estimated flow for the 12 months from October through September of the water year, estimated monthly water yields, constrained estimates of monthly flows, and constrained estimates of monthly yields. The files are written to the subdirectory "..\HSRthsr\Output\FlowYield\"

where "thsr" refers to the four-digit target hydrologic subregion. Filenames are automatically generated to follow the pattern: "QYHSRthsrWYyyyy.csv" where "yyyy" is the four-digit water year.

For the last year in the period of analysis, a comma-delimited file in the directory "..\AFinch\HSRthsr\Output\FlowYield\" named "StationPOA.csv" is written that contains the activity status for historically gaged stations for each year in the analysis. The first line contains labels for the corresponding fields in the second and remaining lines. The first field is the "Site" number that corresponds to the streamgage number and the remaining *Ny* activity status fields are labeled {WY[1],WY[2],...WY[*Ny*]}. An activity status equal to 1 indicates that the corresponding streamgage was active during that water year; 0 indicates that the streamgage was inactive.

Function AccumulateFlows

The function AccumulateFlows is initiated from the main AFINCH GUI by selecting the push button "5. Accumulate Network Flows." The function initiates the script AFConFlowAccum once for each year in the analysis period. For an arbitrary flowline, *Fl*, the accumulated (constrained or unconstrained) flow is symbolized as $\tilde{Q}_{Fl} = \sum_{\hat{n} Fl} \tilde{q}_{Fl}$.

Script AFConFlowAccum

The script AFConFlowAccum (appendix 24) implements the algorithm for accumulating attributes through the NHDPlus network described in the NHDPlus User Guide (U.S. Environmental Protection Agency and U.S. Geological Survey, 2008, p. 45). This involves inputting the "..\HSRthsr\GIS\NHDFlowlineVAA.txt" comma-delimited file. The file contains the fields *ComID*, *FromNode*, *ToNode*, *Hydroseq*, *Divergence*, and *StartFlag* as defined within the NHDFlowlineVAA (dBase) file. In addition, the comma-delimited file contains the *Grid_code* and *AreaSqKm* fields associated with the *ComID*s for the hydrologic subregion of interest. An excerpt from the NHDFlowlineVAA.txt file is shown in figure 26.

The previously computed flows at flowlines and water yields from catchments located at "..\HSRthsr\Output\FlowYield\QYHSRthsrWYyyyy.csv" are read into AFINCH. In addition, the monthly water-use data are read in from the file located at "..\HSRthsr\WaterUse\ComID_WU_All.dat." Flow accumulations are readjusted to add the effects of specified water uses back into the flow network. These accumulated flows also are written to a comma-delimited file with the naming convention "..\HSRthsr\Output\FlowAccum\ComIDQ12WYyyyy.csv." The output file contains a header line identifying the 13 fields in each line of output. These fields are the *ComID* for the corresponding flowline, and

corresponding accumulated monthly flows, $\sum_{\hat{n}} \tilde{q}_{Fl}$, beginning with October and ending with September. All flows are in cubic feet per second.

Function PlotTrendDurations

The function PlotTrendDurations is initiated from the main AFINCH GUI by selecting the push button "6. Plot Trend and Duration Curves." An input dialogue box is opened prompting for the *ComID* of the flowline for which flow-duration and trend analysis is requested. Information for this target *ComID* is read into the workspace, and the script AFTrendDurations is initiated. After the script is completed, control returns to the AFINCH GUI where additional duration and trend analyses can be specified.

Script AFTrendDurations

The script AFTrendDurations (appendix 25) plots monthly flow-duration characteristics and monthly time series of flows for the period of analysis. Flow duration is a continuous function that describes the likelihood that any specified flow magnitude will be exceeded. This function is commonly depicted graphically as a flow-duration curve. The x-axis of this graph provides a measure of the probability of exceedance, and the y-axis depicts the flow magnitude. The curve can be estimated at discrete points from a time series of flow data measured or estimated at fixed intervals, such as hourly, daily, or monthly. For long time series of data, the length of the fixed interval used to compute flow duration has less effect on the middle of the curve than on the ends of the curve. For example, the middle of a flow-duration curve computed from hourly flow data will generally be similar to the flow-duration curve computed from the same hourly data, but aggregated to monthly values. The ends of this curve, say for likelihoods less than 5 percent or greater than 95 percent, will likely differ with the averaging interval.

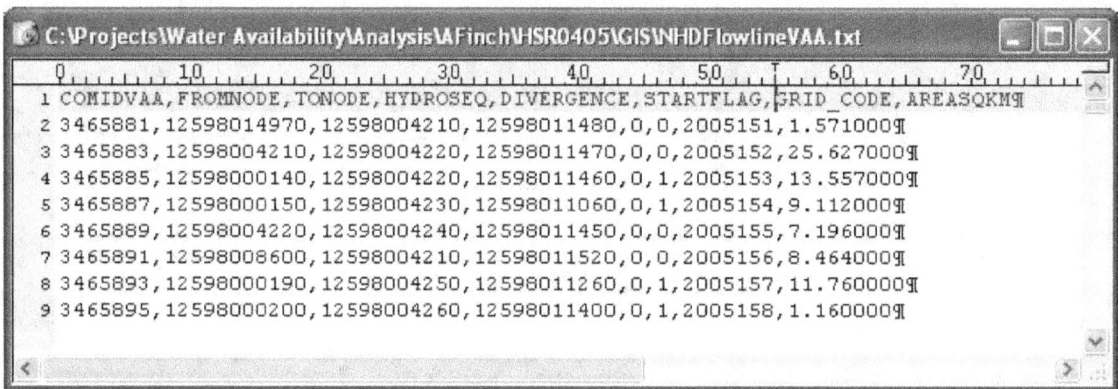

Figure 26. Contents of the NHDFlowlineVAA.txt file for hydrologic subregion 0405.

Interpretation of flow-duration information is contingent on the stationarity of flow, meaning that flow magnitudes are not consistently increasing or decreasing with time. Trends in flow magnitudes limit the utility of flow-duration data because the function represents average conditions over the particular measurement period, rather than conditions that can be expected with a particular probability. The monthly flow-duration graphs that are generated by AFINCH are accompanied by monthly time series plots in which the data are tested for trend.

The script AFTrendDurations reads the flow accumulation file for the period of analysis into the structure variable TrendDurationMatrix, if the variable does not already exist in the workspace. A record in the *ComID* field of the TrendDurationMatrix is sought where the *ComID* matches the user-specified *ComID*. If a matching record is found, flow-duration and trend analyses are initiated. Otherwise, an error dialogue box is displayed indicating that the user-specified *ComID* was found, and control returns to the AFINCH GUI, where the user may respecify a *ComID*.

The script is used to determine whether or not a streamgage was ever located on the target flowline. If so, the period of record for streamgage operation is identified, and corresponding measured monthly flow values are retrieved. Then the ranks are computed for each monthly streamflow value in the period of analysis such that the largest streamflow has a rank of 1 and the smallest streamflow has a rank of *Ny*, the length of the period of analysis. The ranking procedure accommodates tied streamflow magnitudes.

Probability plotting positions (P_i), which estimate the percentage of time monthly flows were equalled or exceeded, are then computed from the ranks (*i*) by use of the Cunnane formula as described by Helsel and Hirsch (2002).

$$P_i = (i - 0.4)/(Ny + 0.2) \qquad (2)$$

The probability plotting positions are scaled to a standard normal probability scale on the x-axis with corresponding flow values plotted as black disks on the logarithmically transformed y-axis (fig. 27). Any measured monthly flows are over plotted as red disks.

The time series of monthly flow values are plotted as black disks for the specified flowline, identified by its *ComID*, through the period of analysis. If a streamgage was operated on the specified flowline during part of the analysis period, the measured flows over plot the constrained estimated flows as

red disks. Each monthly flow series is tested for a monotonic trend using the Mann-Kendall nonparametric test (Helsel and Hirsch, 2002), implemented within the code AFKenSen (appendix 26). Sen's slope estimator (Helsel and Hirsch, 2002) is computed along with an intercept term, which provides a linear description of a monotonic trend. An input dialog box provides a mechanism for specifying the alpha level for the trend test and smoothing parameters, α_1, γ_1, for the moving average smoother, which are discussed below. Summary statistics for significant trends are written to the Matlab command window.

The user specifies whether to describe temporal fluctuations in monthly flows linearly or on the basis of a moving average. If the linear descriptor is specified, significant trends are shown as a solid red line based on Sen's slope estimator and corresponding intercept; for nonsignificant trends, the monthly median flow for the period of analysis is shown as a dashed blue line through the flow series (fig. 28).

If the moving average descriptor of trend is selected, series with significant monotonic trends are depicted by use of a solid red line segment based on a double exponential smoothing of corresponding flows (National Institute of Standards and Technology, 2006). The form of the double exponential smoother is:

$$Z_{iy,im} = \alpha_1 \cdot q_{iy,im} + (1 - \alpha_1) \cdot q_{iy-1,im}$$
$$b_{iy,im} = \gamma_1 \cdot \left(Z_{iy,im} - Z_{iy-1,im}\right) + (1 - \gamma_1) \cdot b_{iy-1,im}, \qquad (3)$$

where

$q_{iy,im}$ is the concurrent monthly flow;

$q_{iy-1,im}$ is the monthly flow 1 year earlier;

$b_{iy,im}$ is the estimate of trend at time $t>1$; and

α_1 and γ_1 are user-specified parameters, which have default values of 0.1.

In AFINCH, $Z_{1,im}$ is the median of the first five values in the monthly flow series ($q_{1,im}, q_{2,im}, \dots q_{5,im}$), and $b_{1,im}$ is the difference between the last and first monthly flow divided by the number of months in the analysis period. Thus, the minimum length of the analysis period for trend analysis is 5 years. If the monotonic trend is not considered significant, a single exponential smoother (National Institute of Standards and Technology, 2006) is plotted as a dashed blue line segment through the monthly flows (fig. 29). The form of the single exponential smoother is $Z_{iy,im} = \alpha_1 \cdot q_{iy-1,im} + (1 - \alpha_1) \cdot Z_{iy-1,im}$.

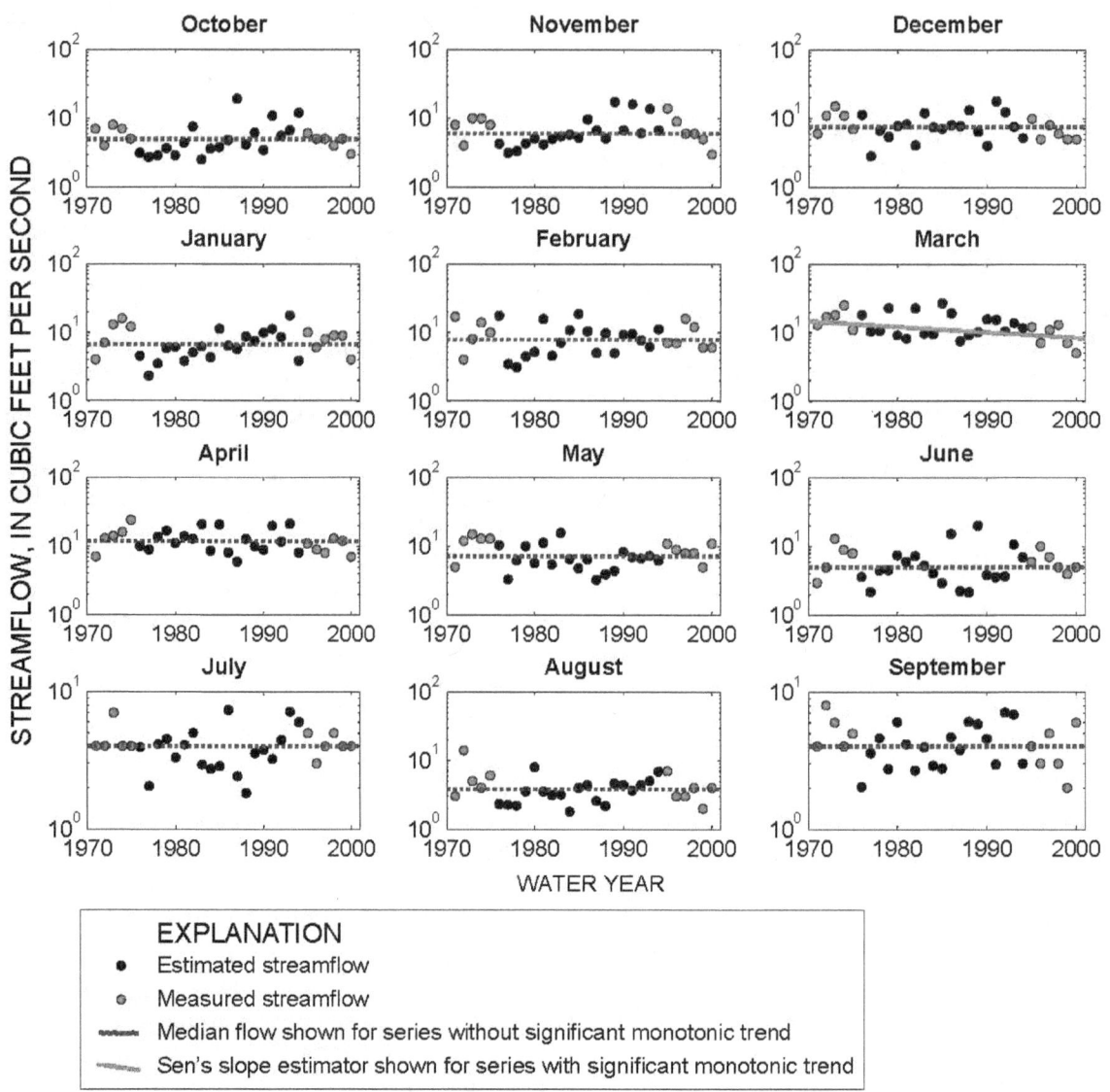

Figure 27. Monthly streamflow-duration characteristics at flowline 12145180 in hydrologic subregion 0405 with measured streamflow at USGS gaging station 04117000 Quaker Brook near Nashville, MI, for water years 1971 to 2000.

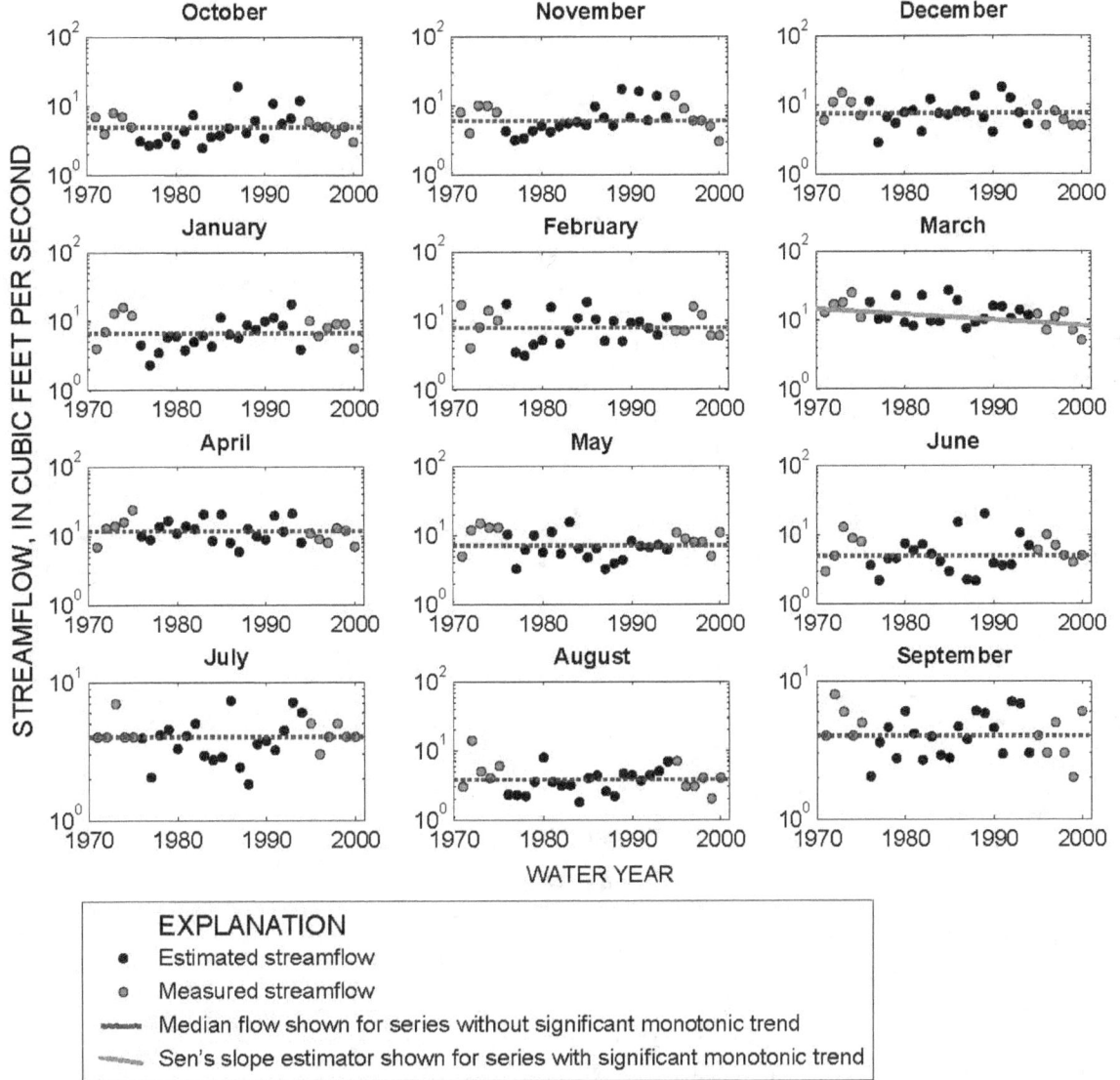

Figure 28.   Monthly flows for water years 1971 to 2000 at the flowline in hydrologic subregion 0405 referenced by the *ComID* 12145180 with measured streamflows at USGS gaging station 04117000 Quaker Brook near Nashville, MI, showing median flows or linear trend components.

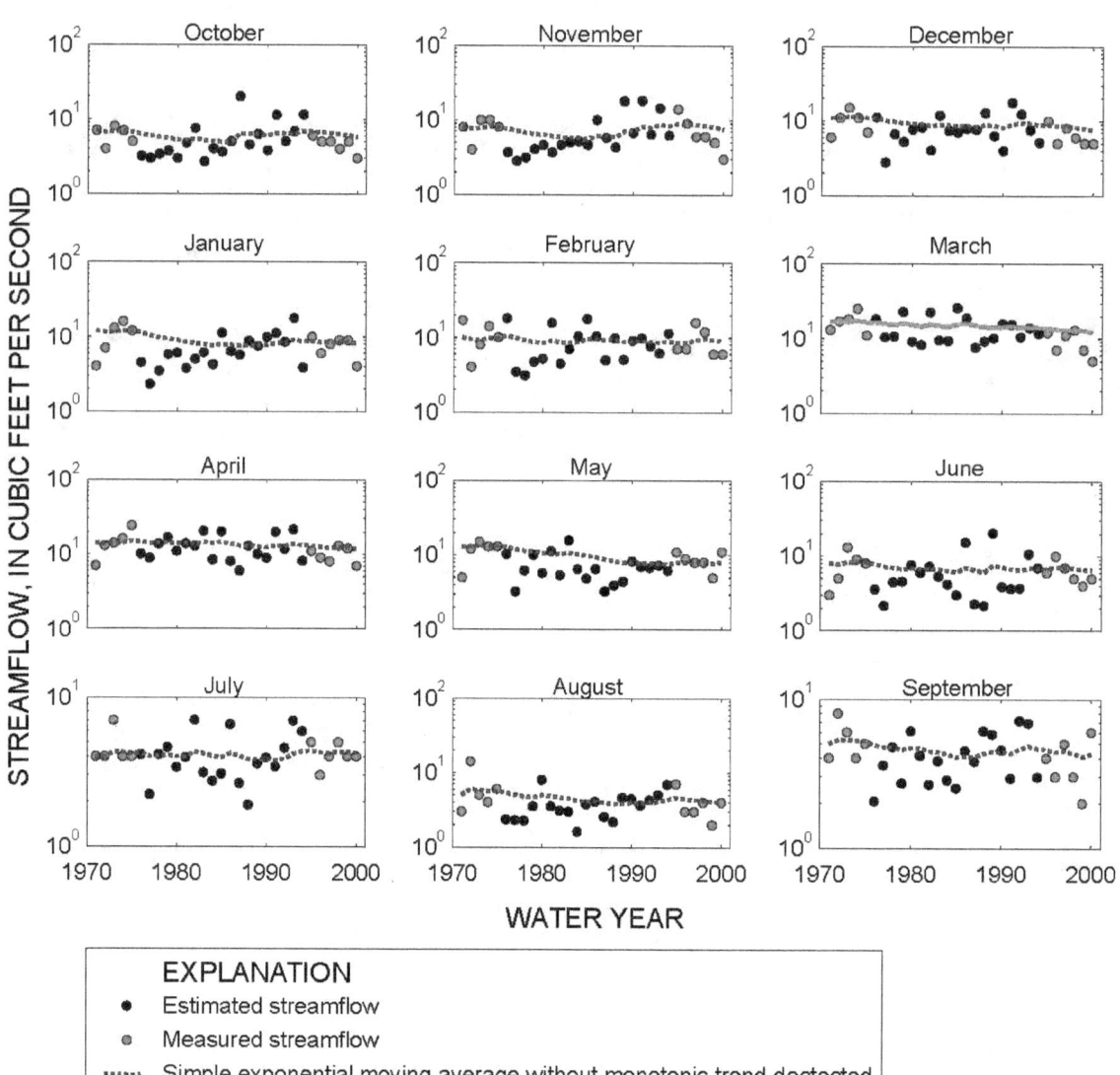

EXPLANATION
- Estimated streamflow
- Measured streamflow
- Simple exponential moving average without monotonic trend dectected
- Double exponential moving average with monotonic trend detected

Figure 29. Monthly flows for water years 1971 to 2000 at the flowline in hydrologic subregion 0405 referenced by the *ComID* 12145180 with measured streamflows at USGS gaging station 04117000 Quaker Brook near Nashville, MI, with moving average smooths.

Function PlotYieldsAtGages

The function PlotYieldsAtGages is initiated by selecting the push button "7. Plot Yields at Streamgages" on the AFINCH GUI. The function provides a mechanism to display monthly water yields across historically gaged basins during the period of analysis. For years outside the period of record at individual streamgages, the estimated water yield is depicted; otherwise, the measured water yield is displayed. In addition, Matlab functionality for interacting with graphs can be used to digitize graph coordinates. These graph coordinates can be exported to the Matlab workspace where corresponding water yields and flows can be determined for the digitized years and stations.

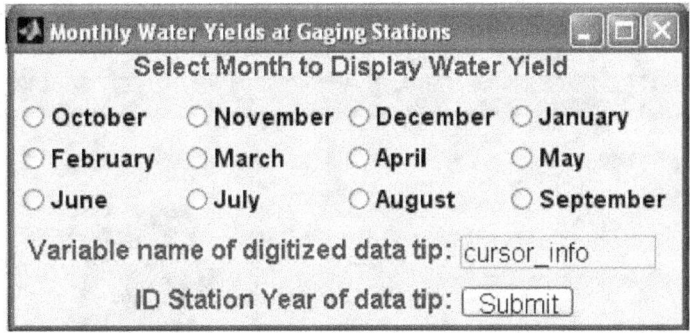

Figure 30. Graphical user interface for selecting the monthly water yields to display for all stations historically gaged during the period of analysis.

Function AFYieldAtGagesGUI

The function PlotYieldsAtGages initiates a GUI script (AFYieldAtGagesGUI, appendix 27) for selecting the month to display measured (or constrained estimates of) water yields at historically gaged locations, Y_s, by clicking on the corresponding radio button (fig. 30). Selecting the month initiates the script AFImagePOAYield (appendix 28), which displays a three-dimensional (3D) bar graph showing the water yields across gaged basins during the period of analysis (fig. 31). The view of the figure can be enlarged or reduced in size, panned, and rotated in 3D by selecting the corresponding shortcut on the Matlab figure toolbar (fig. 32).

The Data Cursor shortcut on the Matlab menu bar at the top of the 3D bar plot of water yields provides a mechanism to identify individual monthly water yields for specific years and streamgages (fig. 32). Once the Data Cursor shortcut is selected, the Matlab cursor changes to a cross hair, and individual 3D bars are identifiable by left clicking. A datatip containing the x, y, and z coordinates of the selected bar is dislayed in a text box near the selected bar. Additional datatips can be created by holding down the "Alternate" (Alt) key and left-clicking additional 3D bars. The datatips for all selected 3D bars can be exported to the Matlab workspace by right-clicking on the figure and choosing the "Export Cursor Data to Workspace…" option from the displayed menu (fig. 32). Once the option is selected, an input dialog box is displayed for entering the variable name of the datatip; the default variable name of "cursor_info" can be used, if desired. The same variable name should be entered in the AFYieldAtGagesGUI

script for selecting the month for which water yields are displayed (fig. 30). Left-clicking on the "Submit" button to the right of the text "ID Station Year of data tip" will identify the selected streamgages and associated flow and water yield statistics. This button runs the script AFid (appendix 29), which writes results (table 3) to the Matlab command window.

The Data Cursor shortcut on the Matlab menu bar at the top of the 3D bar plot of water yields provides a mechanism to identify individual monthly water yields for specific years and streamgages (fig. 32). Once the Data Cursor shortcut is selected, the Matlab cursor changes to a cross hair, and individual 3D bars are identifiable by left clicking. A datatip containing the x, y, and z coordinates of the selected bar is dislayed in a text box near the selected bar. Additional datatips can be created by holding down the "Alternate" (Alt) key and left-clicking additional 3D bars. The datatips for all selected 3D bars can be exported to the Matlab workspace by right-clicking on the figure and choosing the "Export Cursor Data to Workspace…" option from the displayed menu (fig. 32). Once the option is selected, an input dialog box is displayed for entering the variable name of the datatip; the default variable name of "cursor_info" can be used, if desired. The same variable name should be entered in the AFYieldAtGagesGUI script for selecting the month for which water yields are displayed (fig. 30). Left-clicking on the "Submit" button to the right of the text "ID Station Year of data tip" will identify the selected streamgages and associated flow and water yield statistics. This button runs the script AFid (appendix 29), which writes results (table 3) to the Matlab command window.

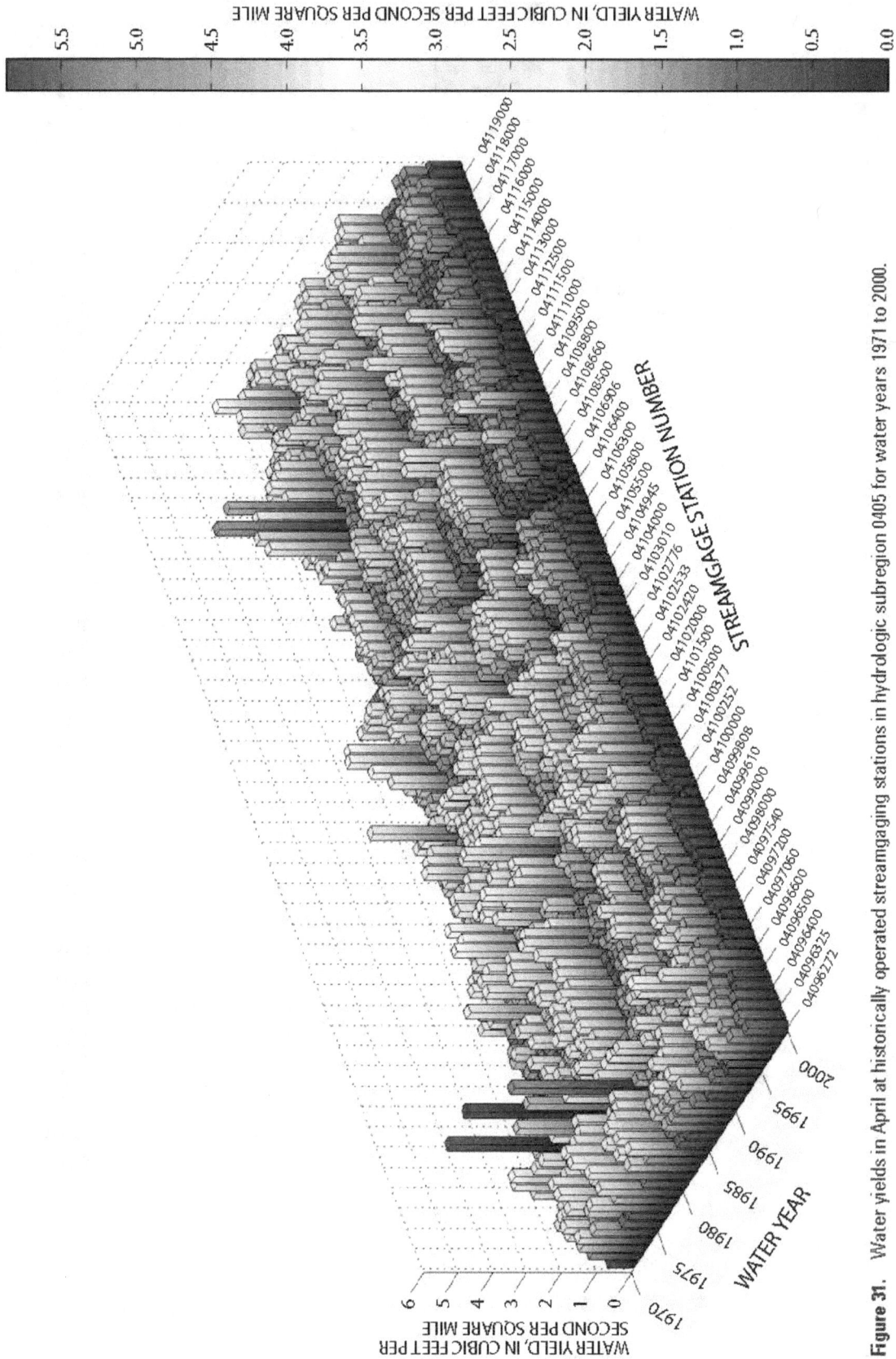

Figure 31.   Water yields in April at historically operated streamgaging stations in hydrologic subregion 0405 for water years 1971 to 2000.

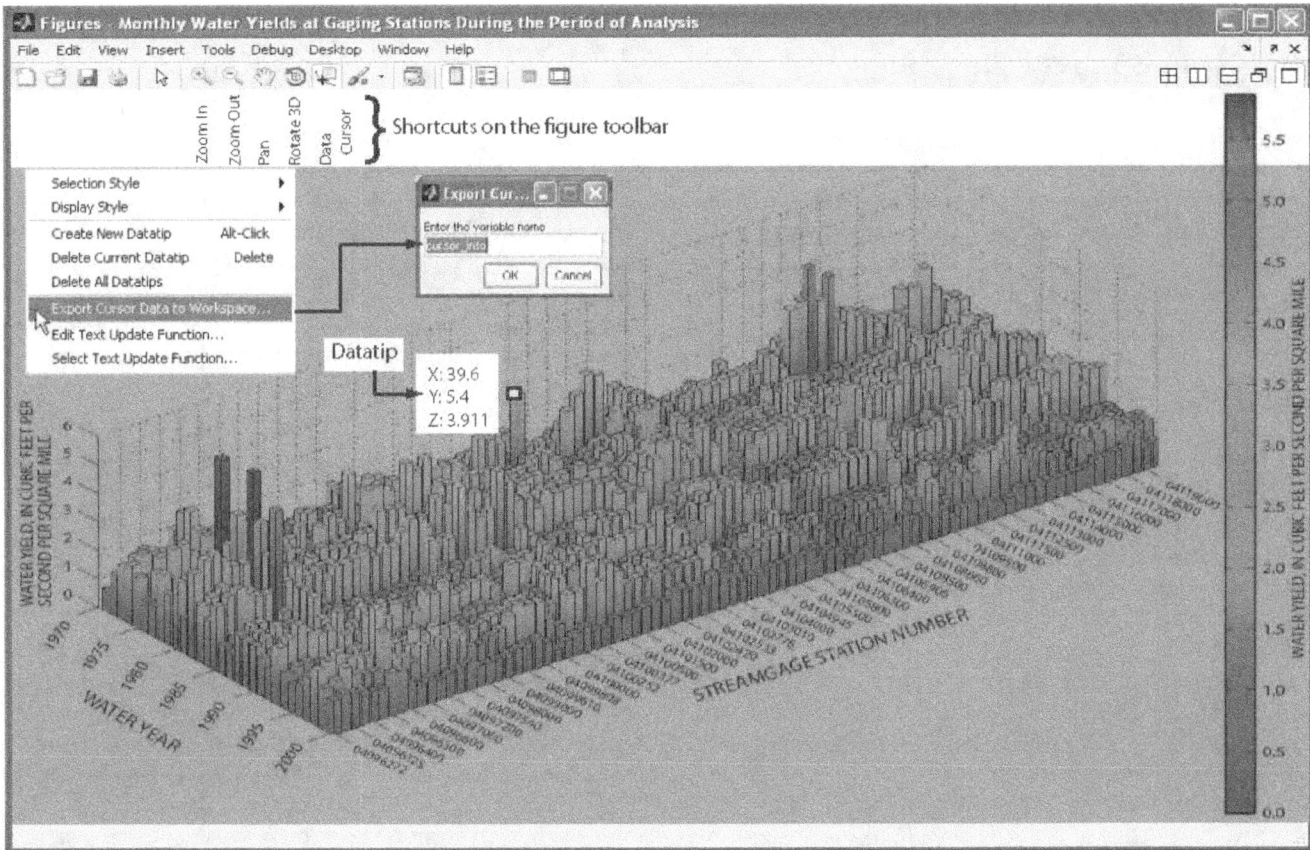

Figure 32. Water yields in April at historically operated streamgaging stations in hydrologic subregion 0405 for water years 1971 to 2000 showing mechanism for exporting water yield information to the Matlab workspace.

Table 3. April flows and water yields for selected streamgages and water years.

USGS station number	Active, T is true, F is false	Month	Water year	Area (square miles)	Flow (cubic feet per second)	Yield (cubic feet per second per square mile)
04102700	T	April	1975	327	83.6	3.91
04106000	F	April	1983	1,999	1,010	1.98
04111500	T	April	1975	65.0	16.3	3.99
04112000	T	April	1975	47.0	9.34	5.03
04112850	F	April	1999	232	80.6	2.88
04117500	T	April	1975	1,433	385	3.72

Mapping Water Yields in Catchments and Streamflow at Flowlines

The following discussion provides an overview of the process needed to integrate AFINCH estimates of water yield at catchments and streamflow at flowlines with the NHDPlus geospatial framework and to display the results in the ESRI GIS programing environment provided by ArcMap. User's manuals for the corresponding system provide detailed instructions and definitions.

Water Yields at Catchments

After initiating ArcMap in the local computing environment, the regional NHDPlus catchment shapefile (catchment.shp) containing the target hydrologic subregion can be added as a data layer. The catchment shapefile commonly occurs in the Drainage folder of the NHDPlus coverage for the hydrologic region of interest, such as "..\NHDPlus04\Drainage\catchment.shp" for hydrologic region 04. The shapefile descibes each catchment as a polygon with associated fields *ComID*, *Grid_Code*, *Grid_count*, *Prod_unit*, and *AreaSqKm* (U.S. Environmental Protection Agency and U.S. Geological Survey, 2008).

Assuming that the first five processes on the AFINCH GUI have been successfully completed for the four-digit target hydrologic subregion (thsr), a comma-delimited output file will have been written to the directory "..\AFinch\HSRthsr\Output\FlowYield\," with the generic name QYHSRthsrWYyyyy.csv, where yyyy is the four-digit water year. The first row of the data file consists of the labels *Grid_Code*, *ComID*, *AreaSqMi* (catchment area in square miles), and four sets of monthly flows, in cubic feet per second, and water yields, in area inches. Estimated monthly flows, adjusted for water use, compose the first 12 fields and are labelled QEstAdjmmm, where mmm is an identifier for the month selected sequentially from the set {Oct,Nov,...,Sep}. The corresponding monthly yields compose the next 12 fields labelled YEstAdjmmm. Finally, constrained estimates of flow, QConAdjmmm, and corresponding yields, YConAdjmmm, make up the remaining 24 columns of data. Within ArcMap, the comma-delimited file can be added as a second data layer.

Within ArcMap, the catchment shapefile can be selected and joined with the flow and yield data on the common *Grid_Code* field. If the join option "Keep only matching records" is selected, catchment geometries outside the target hydrologic subregion will not be displayed. For the joined catchment layer, the symbology (tab) for the layer properties allows selected quantities to be displayed as graduated colors. The color scheme, the number of classes, and the class intervals are user definable. Using this feature, figure 33 shows estimated water yields for May 2000, and figure 34 shows estimates

of water yields constrained by measured flows at active streamgages in May 2000. For the constrained water yields, locations of active streamgages also are shown.

Active streamgages can be displayed in ArcMap by joining the NHDPlus StreamGageEvent shapefile on the *Source_fea* field with the *Site* field in the StationPOA layer (importing the StationPOA.csv file) generated by the Matlab script AFWrtQYEstCon. Selecting the StreamGageEvent layer and using the join option "Keep only matching records" eliminates streamgages outside the target hydrologic subregion. Once joined, records corresponding to an active streamgage for a particular water year can be selected and displayed on the map of water yields or flows.

Streamflow at Flowlines

AFINCH accumulates flows from estimated water yields delivered from catchments and water-use information specified at flowlines to estimate monthly streamflows at all flowlines in the target hydrologic subregion. In gaged basins, flows are constrained by measured flows at active streamgages; elsewhere, flows are based on the user-specified regression for estimating water yields from catchments, their corresponding drainage areas, and water-use data. ArcMap provides a mechanism for displaying and analyzing AFINCH results using the NHDPlus geospatial framework.

The Matlab script AFConFlowAccum generates a set of *Ny* files named ComIDQ12yyyy.csv, where yyyy is a four-digit water year within the period of analysis. Each file contains 13 fields (columns) and as many records (rows) as there are flowlines in the target hydrologic subregion. In addition, the first line of each file provides field labels, which include *ComID* and the corresponding accumulated monthly streamflow as QAccConmmm, where mmm is the abbreviation for the month {Oct,Nov,...,Sep}. The ComIDQ12yyyy.csv files can be imported directly into ArcMap as a layer.

Within ArcMap, the NHDFlowline shapefile can be joined with data in the ComIDQ12yyyy layers by use of the *ComID* field, which is defined in both layers. Flowlines can be symbolized to show monthly flow magnitudes by graduated colors schemes (fig. 35). Individual flowlines can be selected within ArcMap to identify corresponding monthly flow characteristics. The annual streamgage network may be added to faciliate comparison of flow information with measured values. Small discrepancies between measured and accumulated, constrained flows may occur at some streamgages because of the granularity of drainage areas defined within the NHDPlus network. In particular, a streamgage may occur anywhere along the length of a flowline where the drainage area changes continuously. The USGS National Water Information System, NWIS, accounts for this continuous variation. In contrast, NHDPlus drainage areas change discretely between flowlines.

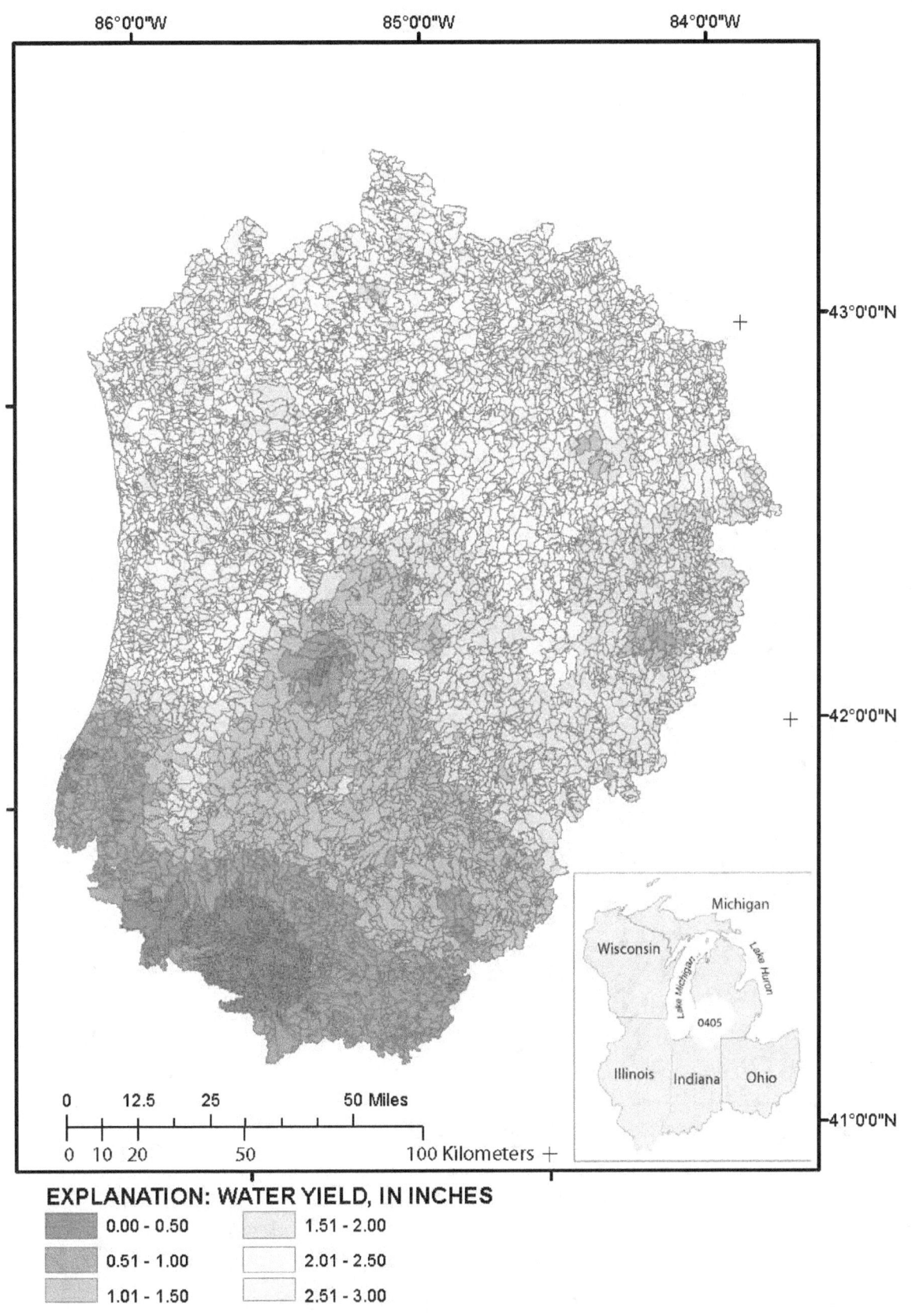

Figure 33.   Estimates of water yields in NHDPlus catchments of hydrologic subregion 0405 in May 2000.

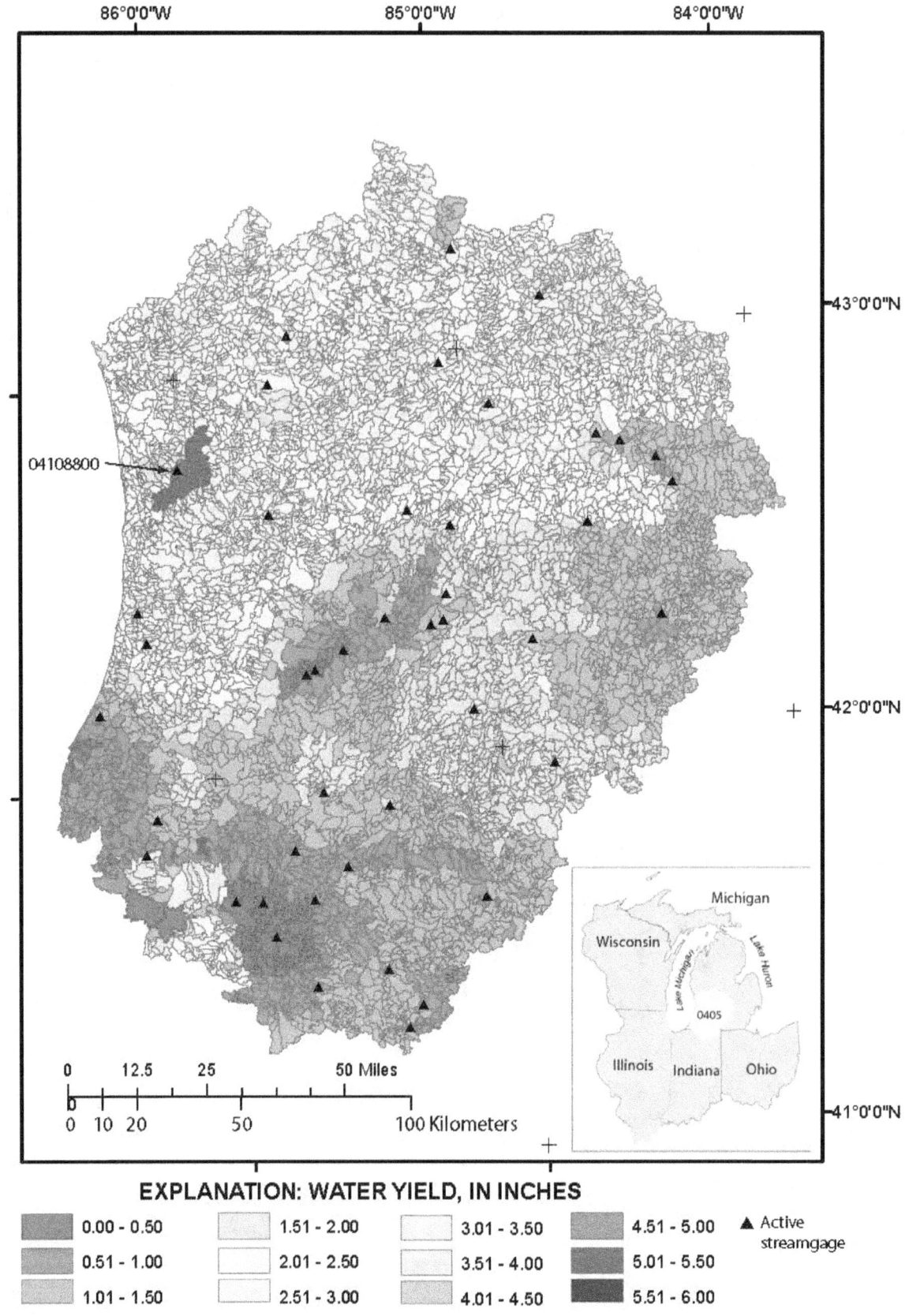

EXPLANATION: WATER YIELD, IN INCHES

0.00 - 0.50	1.51 - 2.00	3.01 - 3.50	4.51 - 5.00
0.51 - 1.00	2.01 - 2.50	3.51 - 4.00	5.01 - 5.50
1.01 - 1.50	2.51 - 3.00	4.01 - 4.50	5.51 - 6.00

▲ Active streamgage

Figure 34.   Estimates of water yields in NHDPlus catchments of hydrologic subregion 0405 constrained by measured flows at streamgages in May 2000.

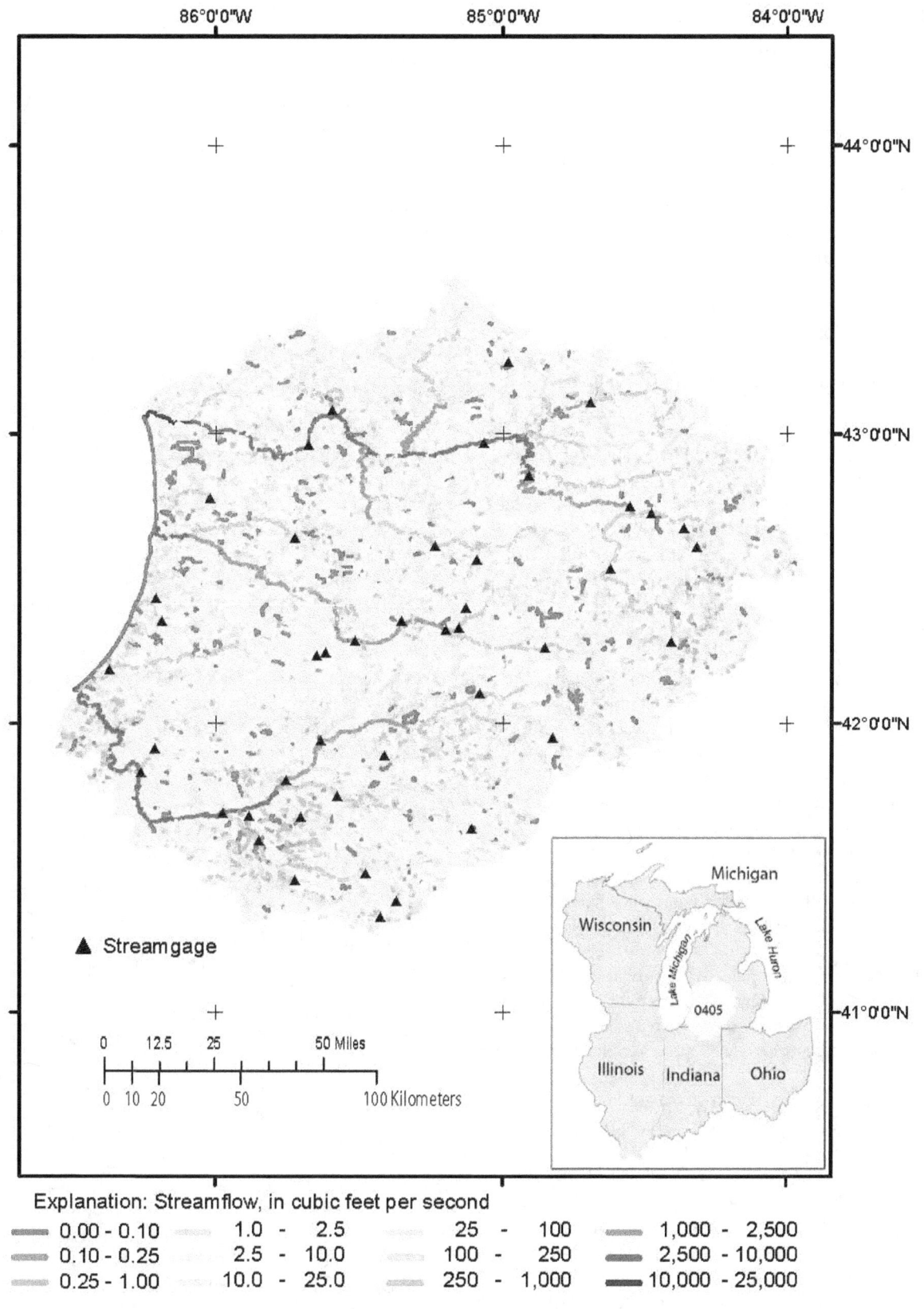

Figure 35.   Estimates of flow at NHDPlus flowlines within hydrologic subregion 0405 constrained by measured flows at streamgages in May 2000.

Limitations of AFINCH and Suggestions for Future Development

AFINCH provides a basis for estimating time series of monthly streamflow and water yields within the NHDPlus geospatial surface-water framework. The estimated flows are consistent with measured flows at active streamgages, and flows are conserved within the network. AFINCH automatically adjusts to annual changes in the active streamgaging network. Monthly water-use data are used to adjust monthly measured flows at streamgages downstream from flowlines of documented withdrawals or augmentations. The adjusted flows provide a basis for improving the estimation of natural water yields from catchments, which are used to develop user-specified multiple regression equation. Anomalies in monthly water-yield images provide a basis for detecting possible deficiencies in water-use data or other factors affecting the expected hydrologic response. Stationarity of monthly streamflow data is not assumed, which provides greater consistency with possible changes in land-use characteristics or climate. Model and data limitations exist, however, providing potential for future development.

AFINCH provides a basis for integrating flow information from the streamgaging network with water-use data. The availability of long-term monthly flowline-specific water-use data, however, is limited. In highly regulated systems affected by water use, interpretation of natural water yields from measured streamflow is problematic in areas of deficient water-use data. Flowline-specific, monthly water-use data are needed to interpret natural water yields in highly regulated systems.

In this report, multiple regression equations for estimating natural water yields were based on monthly climatic data from the PRISM Group and land-cover characteristics described by the NLCD. As of June 2008, however, updates for the monthly climatic data have been suspended because of insufficient funding (http://www.prism. oregonstate.edu/, accessed April 2009). In this report, PRISM precipitation and temperature data were critical to explaining the variability of natural water yields. For future applications, updates to the PRISM data or an alternative source of monthly climatic data would be needed to accurately estimate monthly water yields.

Selected land-cover characteristics based on the NLCD, which are described at the catchment level within NHDPlus, provided significant variables for estimating water yields in this report. Only about 30 percent of the variability in water yields, however, were explained by these equations (fig. 21). Additional geomorphic characteristics, including catchment altitude, slope, and aspect, may be helpful in improving estimation accuracy. These geomorphic characteristics could be determined for each catchment in a nationally consistent manner on the basis of the elevation grid included with NHDPlus. Regionally significant basin characteristics could be defined for each catchment and included among potential explanatory variables in the regression analysis. Such additions would require modification of the GUI used to select explanatory variables in the regression analysis.

Although the multiple regression equations developed in this report had limited ability to estimate water yields, the product of water yields and drainage areas resulted in flow estimates from catchments that described 94 percent of the variability in measured flows (fig. 25). Thus even for ungaged streams, estimation of monthly streamflow is expected to be fairly reliable. For streams with active streamgages, a constraint is applied that proportionally adjusts estimated monthly flows to match measured monthly flows. This constraint essentially eliminates the discrepancy between estimated and measured flow at streamgages and likely reduces the model error at flowlines near a streamgage. Still, any systematic underestimation of the variability of streamflows can degrade the utility of the streamflow estimation results (Hirsch, 1982).

Finally, some topologic connectivity problems were detected in the NHDPlus data for the U.S. Great Lakes hydrologic region. Within ArcMap, tools are available to identify flowlines upstream (or downstream) from any location, along with their corresponding catchment areas. In some places, this connectivity was incomplete, leaving isolated catchments. Although many of these connectivity problems were corrected in hydrologic subregion 0405, they may be unresolved in other areas.

Summary

This report describes the AFINCH application that can be used to estimate a time series of monthly flows and water yields described by the NHDPlus geospatial surface-water framework. In this application, monthly measured flows at streamgages are adjusted on the basis of water-use data to represent natural water yields from corresponding catchments. For ungaged catchments, monthly water yields are estimated on the basis of user-defined multiple-regression equations. Possible explanatory variables include monthly total precipitation and mean air-temperature data from the PRISM Group, and land-use characteristics described by NLCD. Monthly estimates of water yields are used with catchment drainage areas to compute natural flows. Natural flows are adjusted to account for available water-use data, and in basins with active streamgages, constrained to match measured flows at streamgages. Flow is conserved throughout the NHDPlus network. AFINCH dynamically adapts to annual changes in the streamflow monitoring network.

AFINCH generates a time series of estimated monthly flows for NHDPlus flowlines and water yields from catchments. AFINCH can be used to test monthly estimates of flow for trends and compute flow-duration characteristics. This report described concepts associated with the AFINCH application design, as well as data requirements, development techniques, and implementation methods. AFINCH outputs are illustrated by use of data for hydrologic subregion 0405 (Southeastern Lake Michigan), which drains the southwestern corner of Michigan's Lower Peninsula in the U.S. Great Lakes hydrologic region. These results describe preliminary monthly estimates of flow and water yield from 1971 to 2000 at more than 10,000 flowlines and catchments in the subregion. Further development of AFINCH and refinement for flow estimates in subregion 0405 would provide an opportunity to reduce the uncertainty of estimated water yields and flows.

Acknowledgments

The author gratefully acknowledges colleague review comments provided by Robert M. Hirsch, USGS National Research Program, and Greg F. Koltun, USGS Ohio Water Science Center, who provided numerous comments and suggestions that substantially improved the information and clarity of the information. In addition, the author thankfully acknowledges the editorial contributions of Kay E. Hedrick, USGS Enterprise Publishing Network.

Literature Cited

Blumer, S.P., Behrendt, T.E., Ellis, J.M., Minnerick, R.J., LeuVoy,.L., and Whited, C.R., 2001, Water Resources Data Michigan Water Year 2000: U.S. Geological Survey Water-Data Report MI-00-1, 408 p.

Daly, C., and Taylor, G.H., 1998a, United States average monthly or annual precipitation, 1961-90, Corvallis, Oregon; Spatial Climate Analysis Service at Oregon State University (http://www.climatesource.com/cd1/ppt_met_us.html, accessed May 20, 2009).

Daly, C., and Taylor, G.H., 1998b, United States average monthly or annual mean temperature, 1961-90, Corvallis, Oregon; Spatial Climate Analysis Service at Oregon State University.

Hamilton, D.A., Sorrell, R.C., and Holtschlag, D.J., 2008, A regression model for computing index flows describing the median flow for the summer month of lowest flow in Michigan: U.S. Geological Survey Scientific Investigations Report 2008-5096, 43 p.

Helsel, D.R., and Hirsch, R.M., 2002, Statistical methods in water resources: U.S. Geological Survey Techniques of Water-Resources Investigations, book 4, chap. A3, Hydrologic Analysis and Interpretation, 510 p.

Hirsch, R.M., 1982, A comparison of four streamflow record extension techniques: Water Resources Research, v. 18, no. 4, p. 1081-1088.

The MathWorks, 2008a, Matlab Programming Fundamentals, v. 7: Natick, MA, 896 p., accessed January 27, 2009, at http://www.mathworks.com/access/helpdesk/help/pdf_doc/matlab/matlab_prog.pdf

The MathWorks, 2008b, Matlab Statistics Toolbox User's Guide, v. 7: Natick, MA, The MathWorks, Inc., 1749 p., accessed January 27, 2009, at http://www.mathworks.com/access/helpdesk/help/pdf_doc/stats/stats.pdf

Milly, P.C.D., Betancourt, Julio, Falkenmark, Malin, Hirsch, R.M., Kundzewicz, Z.W., Lettenmaier, D.P., and Stouffer, R.J., 2008, Stationarity is dead: Whither water management: Science, v. 319, no. 5863, p. 573-574.

National Institute of Standards and Technology, 2006, Engineering statistics handbook, U.S. Commerce Department, Technology Administration, NIST/SEMATECH e-Handbook of statistical methods, accessed March 12, 2009, at http://www.itl.nist.gov/div898/handbook/pmc/section4/pmc43.htm

U.S. Environmental Protection Agency and the U.S. Geological Survey, 2009 , NHDPlus user guide (January 20), accessed May 15, 2009, at ftp://ftp.horizon-systems.com/NHDPlus/documentation/NHDPLUS_UserGuide.pdf

Seaber, P.R., Kapinos, F.P., and Knapp, G.L., 1987, Hydrologic unit maps: U.S. Geological Survey Water-Supply Paper 2294, 63 p., accessed April 13, 2009, at http://pubs.usgs.gov/wsp/wsp2294/pdf/wsp_2294.pdf

Stapleton, J.H., 1995, Linear Statistical Models: New York, John Wiley, 449 p.

U.S. Geological Survey, 2008, Hydrologic unit maps: What are hydrologic units?: accessed November 24, 2008, at http://water.usgs.gov/GIS/huc.html

Appendixes—Matlab Scripts and Functions for AFINCH

Appendix 1. Starting AFINCH (AFinch)

AFinch is a product of the USGS National Water Availability and Use Program: Great Lakes Pilot. AFinch integrates monthly streamflow data at streamgages, monthly water use data, monthly precipitation and climatic data, and land cover characteristics to estimate monthly flows at NHDPlus flowlines and water yields in catchments within four-digit hydrologic units. David J. Holtschlag, USGS Michigan Water Science Center

- *Startup AFinch Application*

Startup AFinch Application
Determine if AFinch is initiated in the appropriate directory.

```
dir = eval('pwd');
StrtCol = findstr(upper(dir),upper('AFinch\AWork'));
if isempty(StrtCol)
    % If the directory is not appropriate, notify user and end AFinch.
    errordlg('AFinch was not initiated in the ...\AFinch\AWork
subdirectory.',...
        'AFinch Code Not Found.');
    fprintf('Change current directory to ...\\AFinch\\AWork and restart AFinch.
\n');
    return
end
% Determine whether to start new or continue old analysis.
LoadWorkSpace = questdlg('Load Matlab Workspace?',...
    'Continue AFINCH session?','Yes','No','Cancel','No');
switch LoadWorkSpace
    case 'Yes'
        % Clear whatever is in the current workspace
        evalin('base','clear');
        MLws = inputdlg('Enter workspace name:','AFINCH Workspace:');
        assignin('base','MLws',MLws);
        % Load the specified workspace.
        evalin('base','load(MLws{:})');
    case 'No'
        disp('Maintaining workspace.');
    case 'Cancel'
        return
end
%
% Store the current AFinch version
AFVer = '1d';
% Run the AFinch GUI
eval(['AFinchGUI_v',AFVer]);
```

Appendix 2. A Graphical User Interface for AFINCH (AFinchGUI)

AFinch Graphical User Interface: Main Menu

```
function AFinchGUI_v1d
AFVer = evalin('base','AFVer');
%
% Specify GUI size and location on screen
figxpos = 520; figypos = 364; figwdth = 635; fighght = 525;
%
% Initialize the GUI
fhandle = figure(1); clf(fhandle);
% Show program title on figure label
set( fhandle,...
    'Visible','on','Position',[figxpos,figypos,figwdth,fighght],...
    'Color',[.925, .914, .847],'numberTitle','off',...
    'name','USGS: NATIONAL WATER AVAILABILITY AND USE PROPGRAM',...
    'units','pixels','MenuBar','none','ToolBar','Figure');
%
assignin('base','fhandle',fhandle);
%
% Title for AFinch GUI
hTitle.Text = uicontrol('Style','text','FontWeight','bold',...
    'FontSize',18,'ForegroundColor',[0,0,1],...
    'Position',[12,fighght-41,612,32],...
    'HorizontalAlignment','center','String',...
    'AFINCH: Analysis of Flow in Networks of Channels');

TopLine.line = annotation('line',[20 615]./figwdth,...
    [fighght-45,fighght-45]./fighght);

hSubTitle1.Text = uicontrol('Style','text',...
    'String','Target Hydrologic Subregion:',...
    'Position',[40,fighght-79,240,20],'FontSize',12,...
    'FontWeight','bold','HorizontalAlignment','left');

HydroNumber.Edit = uicontrol('Style','edit',...
    'String','Number?','FontSize',10,...
    'Position',[50,fighght-110,140,24],'HorizontalAlignment','left',...
    'Callback',@HydroNumber_Callback);

HydroName.Edit = uicontrol('Style','edit',...
    'String','Name?','FontSize',10,...
    'Position',[240,fighght-110,361,24],'HorizontalAlignment','left',...
    'Callback',@HydroName_Callback);

hSubTitle2.Text = uicontrol('Style','text',...
    'String','Period Of Analysis:',...
    'Position',[40,fighght-151,201,20],'FontSize',12,...
    'FontWeight','bold','HorizontalAlignment','left');

WyStartText.Text = uicontrol('Style','text',...
    'String','Start:',...
    'Position',[50,fighght-182,52,21],'FontSize',12,...
    'FontWeight','normal','HorizontalAlignment','left');

WyStartEdit.Edit = uicontrol('Style','edit',...
    'String','1971?','FontSize',12,...
    'Position',[100,fighght-182,101,21],'HorizontalAlignment','left',...
    'Callback',@WyStartEdit_Callback);

WyEndText.Text = uicontrol('Style','text',...
    'String','End:',...
    'Position',[240,fighght-182,52,21],'FontSize',12,...
    'FontWeight','normal','HorizontalAlignment','left');
```

```
WyEndEdit.Edit = uicontrol('Style','edit',...
    'String','2010?','FontSize',12,...
    'Position',[280,fighght-182,101,21],'HorizontalAlignment','left',...
    'Callback',@WyEndEdit_Callback);

MidLine.line = annotation('line',[20 615]./figwdth,...
    [fighght-195,fighght-195]./fighght);

CompileData.PushButton = uicontrol('Style','pushbutton','FontSize',12,...
    'String','1. Compile Data','FontSize',10,'HorizontalAlignment','left',...
    'Position',[20,fighght-235,220,26],'HorizontalAlignment','left',...
    'Callback',@CompileData_Callback);

SpecifyRegression.PushButton =
uicontrol('Style','pushbutton','FontSize',12,...
    'String','2. Specify Regression Form','FontSize',10,...
    'Position',[20,fighght-275,220,26],'HorizontalAlignment','left',...
    'Callback',@SpecifyRegression_Callback);

RunRegression.PushButton = uicontrol('Style','pushbutton','FontSize',12,...
    'String','3. Run Annual Regressions','FontSize',10,...
    'Position',[20,fighght-315,220,26],'HorizontalAlignment','left',...
    'Callback',@RunRegression_Callback);

ComputeFlows.PushButton = uicontrol('Style','pushbutton','FontSize',12,...
    'String','4. Compute Incremental Flows','FontSize',10,...
    'Position',[20,fighght-355,220,26],'HorizontalAlignment','left',...
    'Callback',@ComputeFlows_Callback);

AccumulateFlows.PushButton = uicontrol('Style','pushbutton','FontSize',12,...
    'String','5. Accumulate Network Flows','FontSize',10,...
    'Position',[20,fighght-395,220,26],'HorizontalAlignment','left',...
    'Callback',@AccumulateFlows_Callback);

PlotTrendDurations.PushButton =
uicontrol('Style','pushbutton','FontSize',12,...
    'String','6. Plot Trend and Duration Curves','FontSize',10,...
    'Position',[20,fighght-435,220,26],'HorizontalAlignment','left',...
    'Callback',@PlotTrendDurations_Callback);

PlotYieldsAtGages.PushButton =
uicontrol('Style','pushbutton','FontSize',12,...
    'String','7. Plot Yields at Streamgages','FontSize',10,...
    'Position',[20,fighght-475,220,26],'HorizontalAlignment','left',...
    'Callback',@PlotYieldsAtGages_Callback);

hVerNumber.Text = uicontrol('Style','text',...
    'String',['v. ',AFVer],...
    'Position',[7,fighght-515,30,10],'FontSize',8);

CloseButton.PushButton = uicontrol('Style','pushbutton','FontSize',12,...
    'String','Close','FontSize',10,...
    'Position',[540,fighght-515,50,26],'HorizontalAlignment','left',...
    'Callback',@CloseButton_Callback);
%
```

```
function HydroNumber Callback(gcf, event data, HydroNumber)
HydroNumber.THS = get(gcf,'String');
assignin('base','THS',HydroNumber.THS);
fprintf(1,'HydroNumber: %s \n',HydroNumber.THS);
%
function HydroName_Callback(gcf, event_data, HydroName)
HydroName.THSName = get(gcf,'String');
assignin('base','THSName',HydroName.THSName);
fprintf(1,'HydroNumber: %s \n',HydroName.THSName);
%
function WyStartEdit Callback(gcf, event data, WyStartEdit)
WyStartEdit.WY1 = str2double(get(gcf,'String'));
assignin('base','WY1',WyStartEdit.WY1);
fprintf(1,'Start WY: %u\n',WyStartEdit.WY1);
%
function WyEndEdit_Callback(gcf, event_data, WyEndEdit)
WyEndEdit.WYn = str2double(get(gcf,'String'));
assignin('base','WYn',WyEndEdit.WYn);
fprintf(1,'End WY:   %u\n',WyEndEdit.WYn);
%
function CloseButton Callback(gcf, event data, CloseButton)
button = questdlg('Save Matlab Workspace?','Leaving AFINCH','Yes','No','No');
switch button
    case 'Yes'
        MLws = inputdlg('Enter filename to store workspace','Storing
Workspace');
        assignin('base','MLws',MLws);
        evalin('base','save(MLws{:})');
    case 'No'
        msgbox('Leaving AFINCH without saving workspace','help');
end
evalin('base','close(fhandle)');
%
function CompileData_Callback(gcf, eventdata, CompileData)
% Step 1. Compile Data
WY1 = evalin('base','WY1');
WYn = evalin('base','WYn');
fhandle = evalin('base','fhandle');
CompileData.Ny = WYn - WY1 + 1;
assignin('base','Ny',CompileData.Ny);
%
CompileData.button = 'Continue';
evalin('base','AFIniAFStruct v1d');
% Read in precipitation for prior year
CompileData.WY = WY1 - 1;
assignin('base','WY',CompileData.WY);
evalin('base','AFReadNLCD v1d');
evalin('base','AFReadPrismPrec v1d');
%
for iy=1:CompileData.Ny,
    figure(fhandle);
    annotation('rectangle',[.38,.55000,.58*iy/CompileData.Ny,.051],...
        'FaceColor',[.5,.5,.5]);
    assignin('base','iy',iy);
    evalin('base','AFSetupData v1d');
    if strcmp(CompileData.button,'Continue')
        button = questdlg(['Continue to water year ',num2str(WY1+iy),...
```

```
                      ', overwritting graphs.'],'Overwrite graphs?',...
                  'Overwrite current','Review','Overwrite all','Continue');
            switch button
                case {'Overwrite current','Yes'}
                    disp('Continuing...');
                case 'Review'
                    disp('Press any key to continue.')
                    pause
                case 'Overwrite all'
                    CompileData.button = 'Skip';
                    disp('Continuing for all');
            end
    end
end
evalin('base','AFGenLag1Precp v1d');
%
function SpecifyRegression_Callback(gcf, event_data, SpecifyRegression)
% Step 2. Specify Regression Form
SpecifyRegression.Nr = inputdlg( {'Number of Explanatory Variables in
Regression?'},...
        'Specify Number of Explanatory Variables',1,{'3'});
fprintf(1,'Number of variables %s\n',SpecifyRegression.Nr{1});
Nr = str2double(SpecifyRegression.Nr{1});
assignin('base','Nr',Nr);
evalin('base','AFBoxplotExplanVar v1d');
fhandle = evalin('base','fhandle');
for ir=1:str2double(SpecifyRegression.Nr{1}),
    figure(fhandle);
    annotation('rectangle',[.38,.47500,.58*ir/Nr,.051],...
        'FaceColor',[.5,.5,.5]);
    assignin('base','ir',ir);
    evalin('base','AFCallRegCheckBox v1d');
end
evalin('base','AFRegressPOA v1d');

function RunRegression_Callback(gcf, eventdata, RunRegression)
% Step 3.  Run Annual Regressions
global iy
WY1 = evalin('base','WY1');
WYn = evalin('base','WYn');
fhandle = evalin('base','fhandle');
RunRegression.Ny = WYn - WY1 + 1;
annotation('Textbox','Position',[.38,.40000,.58,.051],...
    'String','Running...','HorizontalAlignment','Right');
RunRegression.button1 = 'Overwrite current';
%
for iy=1:RunRegression.Ny,
    figure(fhandle);
    annotation('rectangle',[.38,.40000,.58*iy/RunRegression.Ny,.051],...
        'FaceColor',[.5,.5,.5]);
    % assignin('base','iy',iy);
    evalin('base','AFRegressByWY v1d');
    if ~strcmp(RunRegression.button1,'Overwrite all')
        RunRegression.button1 = questdlg(['Continue to water year ',...
            num2str(WY1+iy),...
            ', overwritting graphs.'],'Overwrite graphs?',...
            'Overwrite current','Review','Overwrite all',...
```

```
                    'Overwrite current');
        switch RunRegression.button1
            case {'Overwrite current','Yes'}
                disp('Continuing...');
            case 'Review'
                disp('Press any key to continue.')
                pause
            case 'Overwrite all'
                RunRegression.button1 = 'Overwrite all';
                disp('Continuing for all');
        end
    end
end
RunRegression.button2 = 'Overwrite current';
for im=1:12,
    assignin('base','im',im);
    evalin('base','AFPlotRegressCoeff_v1d');
    if ~strcmp(RunRegression.button2,'Overwrite all')
        RunRegression.button2 = questdlg(['Continue to water year ',...
            num2str(WY1+iy),...
            ', overwritting graphs.'],'Overwrite graphs?',...
            'Overwrite current','Review','Overwrite all',...
            'Overwrite current');
        switch RunRegression.button2
            case {'Overwrite current','Yes'}
                disp('Continuing...');
            case 'Review'
                disp('Press any key to continue.')
                pause
            case 'Overwrite all'
                RunRegression.button2 = 'Overwrite all';
                disp('Continuing for all');
        end
    end

end
%
function ComputeFlows Callback(gcf, eventdata, ComputeFlows)
% Step 4.  Compute Incremental Flows
global iy
fhandle = evalin('base','fhandle');
Ny   = evalin('base','Ny');
nTHS = evalin('base','nTHS');
Nr   = evalin('base','Nr');
WY1  = evalin('base','WY1');
assignin('base','YEstAdjInc',zeros(Ny,nTHS,12));
assignin('base','QEstAdjInc',zeros(Ny,nTHS,12));
assignin('base','OnesVector',ones(nTHS,1));
assignin('base','RegDesign',zeros(nTHS,Nr));
annotation('Textbox','Position',[.38,.32200,.58,.051],...
    'String','Running...','HorizontalAlignment','Right');
% Initialize starting water year for loop
assignin('base','WY',WY1-1);
for iy=1:Ny,
    evalin('base','AFQEstAdjInc v1d');
end
annotation('rectangle',[.38,.32200,.58*1/4,.051],...
```

```
        'FaceColor',[.5,.5,.5]);
YEstAdjInc = evalin('base', 'YEstAdjInc');
assignin('base','YConAdjInc',YEstAdjInc);
QEstAdjInc  = evalin('base',  'QEstAdjInc');
assignin('base','QConAdjInc',QEstAdjInc);
% Initialize starting water year for loop
% assignin('base','iy',0);
for iy=1:Ny,
    evalin('base','AFQConAdjInc vld');
end
annotation('rectangle',[.38,.32200,.58*2/4,.051],...
    'FaceColor',[.5,.5,.5]);
% Plot Measured and Estimated Qm values
% Initialize starting water year for loop
assignin('base','WY',WY1-1);
ComputeFlows.button = 'Overwrite current';
% Plot measured and estimated flows each year
for iy=1:Ny,
    evalin('base','AFPlotQmMeaEst vld');
    if ~strcmp(ComputeFlows.button,'Overwrite all')
        button = questdlg(['Continue to water year ',num2str(WY1+iy),...
            ', overwritting graphs.'],'Overwrite graphs?',...
            'Overwrite current','Review','Overwrite all',...
            'Overwrite current');
        switch button
            % Overwrites if first button is selected or keyboard return
            case {'Overwrite current','Yes'}
                disp('Continuing...');
            case 'Review'
                disp('Press any key to continue.')
                pause
            case 'Overwrite all'
                ComputeFlows.button = 'Overwrite all';
                disp('Continuing for all');
            case {}
                break
        end
    end
end
annotation('rectangle',[.38,.32200,.58*3/4,.051],...
    'FaceColor',[.5,.5,.5]);
% Read in initial starting year from MATLAB workspace
assignin('base','WY',WY1-1);
fprintf(1,'assignin(base),WY= %4.0f\n',WY1-1);
for iy=1:Ny,
    evalin('base','AFWrtQYEstCon vld');
    figure(fhandle);
%       annotation('rectangle',[.38,.26804,.58*iy/Ny,.051],...
%            'FaceColor',[.5,.5,.5]);
end
annotation('rectangle',[.38,.32200,.58,.051],...
    'FaceColor',[.5,.5,.5]);
%
function AccumulateFlows Callback(gcf, event data, AccumulateFlows)
% Step 5. Accumulate Network Flows
global iy
fhandle = evalin('base','fhandle');
```

```
% Read in the Hydrologic Subregion from the MATLAB workspace
HSR = evalin('base','HSR');
% Define the matrix X in the MATLAB workspace
assignin('base','X',csvread(['..\',HSR,'\GIS\NHDFlowLineVAA.txt'],1));
WY1 = evalin('base','WY1');
Ny = evalin('base','Ny');
AccumulateFlows.button = 'Overwrite current';
annotation('Textbox','Position',[.38,.24600,.58,.051],...
    'String','Running...','HorizontalAlignment','right');
for iy=1:Ny,
    evalin('base','AFConFlowAccum_v1d');
    figure(fhandle);
    annotation('rectangle',[.38,.24600,.58*iy/Ny,.051],...
        'FaceColor',[.5,.5,.5]);
%    Code commented because it is not needed if constrained flows are not
%    plotted in AFConFlowAccum
%    if ~strcmp(AccumulateFlows.button,'Overwrite All');
%        button = questdlg(['Continue to water year ',num2str(WY1+iy-1),...
%            ', overwritting graphs.'],'Overwrite graph?',...
%            'Overwrite current','Review','Overwrite All','Overwrite
current');
%        switch button
%            case {'Overwrite current','Yes'}
%                disp('Overwriting...');
%            case 'Review'
%                disp('Press any key to continue.');
%                pause
%            case 'Overwrite All'
%                disp('Overwriting all...');
%                AccumulateFlows.button = 'Overwrite All';
%        end
%    end
end
%
function PlotTrendDurations Callback(gcf, event data, PlotTrendDurations)
% Step 6. Plot Trend and Duration Curves
PlotTrendDurations.ComID = inputdlg('Enter ComID for Selected Flowline:',...
    'Duration and Trend Analysis');
PlotTrendDurations.ComIDTarget = str2double(PlotTrendDurations.ComID{1});
fprintf(1,'Selected ComID number is %u.\n',PlotTrendDurations.ComIDTarget);
assignin('base','ComIDTarget',PlotTrendDurations.ComIDTarget);
evalin('base','AFTrendDurations_v1d');
%
function PlotYieldsAtGages Callback(gcf, event data, PlotYieldsAtGages)
% Step 7. Plot Water Yields at Streamgages for the Period of Analysis
evalin('base','AFYieldAtGagesGUI_v1d');
```

Appendix 3. Initialize Common Variables in the Matlab Workspace (AFIniAFStruct)

- *Initialize common variables in the MATLAB workspace.*
- *Set common parameters for figures.*
- *Initialize structure for the Target Hydrologic Subregion.*

Initialize common variables in the MATLAB workspace.

```
HSR     = ['HSR',THS];
% Month name
MonthName = {'October','November','December','January','February',...
    'March','April','May','June','July','August','September'};
%
% Abbreviated month name
MoName = {'Oct.','Nov.','Dec.','Jan.','Feb.','Mar.','Apr.','May','June',...
    'July','Aug.','Sep.'};
%
% Calendar month sequency in water year
MoNumber = [10:12 1:9];
%
```

Set common parameters for figures.

```
set(0,'units','pixels');
get(0,'CurrentFigure');
set(gcf,'units','pixels');
screenrect = get(0,'screensize');
screenwidth = screenrect(3); screenheight = screenrect(4);
figwidth = 1100; figheight = 700;
figposition = [(screenwidth/2-figwidth/2)...
    (screenheight/2-figheight/2)...
    figwidth figheight];
%
```

Initialize structure for the Target Hydrologic Subregion

```
AFstruct.(HSR)   = struct([]);
```

Appendix 4. Setup Data for AFINCH (AFSetupData)

Contents

```
disp('<a href="matlab: junk=0;">AFSetupData</a>');
% Run sequence of Matlab scripts to setup data structures
% Clear Command Window
clc
% Update water year
WY = WY1 + iy -1;
%
% Days In Month is variable handle leap years
DaysInMo = [31 30 31 31 eomday(WY,2) 31 30 31 30 31 31 30 337+eomday(WY,2)];
%
fprintf(1,'-----------------------------------------------------------------
-\n');
fprintf(1,'  AFINCH: Analysis of Flow in Networks of Channels for Water
Year\n');
fprintf(1,'    %s in Target Hydrologic Subregion (THS) %s\n',num2str(WY),THS);
fprintf(1,'-----------------------------------------------------------------
-\n');
%
% Run scripts
```

AFReadNLCD

Read in NLCD data
```
eval(['AFReadNLCD_v',AFVer]);
```
AFReadPrismPrec

Read in PRISM precipitation and temperature data
```
eval(['AFReadPrismPrec_v',AFVer]);
```
AFGenStrucData

Create data structure that contains ComIDs, GridCodes, Stations, for all historical stationsin the
THS. Uses a StationList.txt file and csv files generated from ArcMap for each station.
```
eval(['AFGenStrucData_v',AFVer]);
```
AFReadInFlowWY

Read in WY specific flows at gaging stations and non-WY specific water use data.
```
eval(['AFReadInFlowWY_v',AFVer]);
```
AFStaBasinGridComIDWY

Generate data files
```
eval(['AFStaBasinGridComIDWY_v',AFVer]);
```
AFPlotAreaFlows

Plots a 4x3 array of monthly incremental measured and adjusted flows and drainage areas for
gaging stations in the WY.
```
eval(['AFPlotAreasFlows_v',AFVer]);
```
AFYieldImage

Plots an image of incremental water yield by month for measured flows and flows adjusted for
water use.
```
eval(['AFYieldImage_v',AFVer]);
```
AFReadPrismTemp

Read in PRISM Temperature and Precipitation data, compute weighted average for active
stations, store results in HSR file structure
```
eval(['AFReadPrismTemp_v',AFVer]);
```

Appendix 5. Read in National Land Cover Data (AFRead NLCD)

- *Reading in region data sets*
- *Extracting the specified subregional data and joining data*
- *Intersecting the nhdflowline and NLCD data sets*
- *Deleting variables that are no longer needed*

Reading in region data sets

```
disp('<a href="matlab: junk=0;">AFReadNLCD</a>');
fprintf('\n AFReadNLCD: Reading NLCD data for hydrologic region
HSR%s00.\n',THS(1:2));
% Note: The "catchmentattributesnlcd.txt" file read below can be
% created by adding the "NHDPlus##\catchmentattributesnlcd.dbf"
% data file to an ArcMap session, where '##' is (generally) a two-
% digit code identifying Hydrologic Region number of interest.
% Once the table is in ArcMap, it can be exported as a comma
% delimited text (txt) file. Leading commas in column 1 and the
% decimal and tailing zeros in the first two fields (ComID and
% GridCode) must be eliminated before reading the data with
% format string below because these fields are read as integers (%u).
[ComID NLCD,GridCode NLCD,NLCD11,NLCD12,NLCD21,NLCD22,...
    NLCD23,NLCD31,NLCD32,NLCD33,NLCD41,NLCD42,NLCD43,...
    NLCD51,NLCD61,NLCD71,NLCD81,NLCD82,NLCD83,NLCD84,...
    NLCD85,NLCD91,NLCD92,PCTCN,PCTMX,SUMPCT]=...
    textread(['..\HSR',THS(1:2),'00\NLCD\catchmentattributesnlcd.txt'],...
    ['%u%u',repmat('%f',1,24)],...
    'delimiter',',','headerlines',1);
%
% Determine the number of records in the NLCD catchment dataset
lenNLCD = length(unique(ComID NLCD));
fprintf(1,[' %u unique ComIDs were read from the 1992 NLCD ',...
    'for hydrologic region %s.\n'],lenNLCD,THS(1:2));
%
%
fprintf('\n Reading the nhdflowline data for the region.\n');
% Note: The "nhdflowline.txt" file read below can be
% created by adding the "NHDPlus##\Hydrography\nhdflowline.shp
% shape file to an ArcMap session.  Once the attribute table associated
% with the shape file is opened in ArcMap, fields other than "COMID",
% "LENGTHKM", AND "REACHCODE" can be turned off to prevent their
% display and export. The selected fields can then be exported
% by selecting the appropriate options for exporting a text file
% within the table view of ArcMap. The double quotes around the
% REACHCODE should be deleted before reading the file into MATLAB
% with the command below.
%
% Read in ComID,LengthKm,ReachCode for Hydrologic Region
[ComID NHDFlowLine, LengthKm, ReachCode] = textread(...
    ['..\HSR',THS(1:2),'00\Flowlines\nhdflowline.txt'],...
    '%u %f %s','delimiter',',','headerlines',1);
%
% Determine the number of flowline records
lenNHDFlowLine = length(unique(ComID_NHDFlowLine));
fprintf(1,[' %u unique ComIDs were read from the nhdflowline file ',...
    'for hydrologic region %s.\n'],lenNHDFlowLine,THS(1:2));

% Compare the number of flowlines with catchments
fprintf(1,[' There are %u fewer (%4.1f percent) ComIDs associated ',...
    'with catchments than there are \n'],...
    lenNHDFlowLine-lenNLCD, (lenNHDFlowLine-lenNLCD)/lenNLCD*100 );
fprintf(1,'       ComIDs assoicated with nhdflowlines in the region.\n');
%
```

Extracting the specified subregional data and joining data

Ind is an 0/1 indicator vector of the subregion in the ReachCode

```
Ind = strncmp(ReachCode,THS,4);

% Ndx is the subset of indices for the subregion in the regional data
Ndx = find(Ind==1);

% ComID and ReachCodes for the specified subregion
ComID THSFlowLine    = ComID NHDFlowLine(Ndx);
lenComID THSFlowLine = length(ComID THSFlowLine);
ReachCodeTHSFlowLine = ReachCode(Ndx);
%
```

Intersecting the nhdflowline and NLCD data sets

```
[junk,NdxA,NdxB]     = intersect(ComID THSFlowLine,ComID NLCD);
n                    = length(NdxB);
ComID THSNLCD        = ComID NLCD(NdxB);
lenComID THSNLCD     = length(ComID THSNLCD);
%
fprintf(1,['  There are %u (%4.1f percent) fewer ComIDs associated ',...
    'with catchments than \n'],...
    lenComID THSFlowLine-lenComID THSNLCD,...
    (lenComID THSFlowLine-lenComID THSNLCD)/...
    lenComID THSNLCD*100);
fprintf(1,'    ComIDs associated with NDHFlowLines in HSR%s.\n',THS);

GridCode THSNLCD = GridCode NLCD(NdxB);
NLCD11THS = NLCD11(NdxB); NLCD12THS = NLCD12(NdxB); NLCD21THS = NLCD21(NdxB);
NLCD22THS = NLCD22(NdxB); NLCD23THS = NLCD23(NdxB); NLCD31THS = NLCD31(NdxB);
NLCD32THS = NLCD32(NdxB); NLCD33THS = NLCD33(NdxB); NLCD41THS = NLCD41(NdxB);
NLCD42THS = NLCD42(NdxB); NLCD43THS = NLCD43(NdxB); NLCD51THS = NLCD51(NdxB);
NLCD61THS = NLCD61(NdxB); NLCD71THS = NLCD71(NdxB); NLCD81THS = NLCD81(NdxB);
NLCD82THS = NLCD82(NdxB); NLCD83THS = NLCD83(NdxB); NLCD84THS = NLCD84(NdxB);
NLCD85THS = NLCD85(NdxB); NLCD91THS = NLCD91(NdxB); NLCD92THS = NLCD92(NdxB);
%
fprintf(1,'  Selected %u records for hydrologic subregion HSR%s from
hydrologic region %s.\n',...
    n,THS,THS(1:2));
```

Deleting variables that are no longer needed.

```
clear PCTCN PCTMX SUMPCT ComID NLCD ComID USGL
clear NLCD11 NLCD12 NLCD21 NLCD22 NLCD23 NLCD31 NLCD32 NLCD33 NLCD41
clear NLCD42 NLCD43 NLCD51 NLCD61 NLCD71 NLCD81 NLCD82
clear NLCD83 NLCD84 NLCD85 NLCD91 NLCD92
clear GridCode NLCD Ind LengthKm ReachCode
clear ReachCodeTHS lenNHDFlowLine lenNLCD junk
clear Ndx NdxA NdxB nTHS
clear ia ib n ComID IntTHSNLCD ComID MisTHSNLCD GridCode IntTHSNLCD
clear PCTCN PCTMX SUMPCT
```

Appendix 6. Read in PRISM Precipitation Data (AFReadPrismPrec)

Contents
- *Read in PRISM Precipitation Data for the Water Year*
- *Intersect GridCodes and ComIDs in Target Hydrologic Subregion*
- *Match Corresponding Records in NLCD and Prism Precipitation*
- *Clear Variables*

AFReadPrismPrec reads in ASCII files of precipitation data. Creation of these data files requires extensive GIS processing. In this analysis, monthly precipitation data was obtained from PRISM data sets. PRISM (Parameter-elevation Regressions on Independent Slopes Model) data sets are available as gridded data with a cell size of 2.5-arcmin or about 4 km on a side.

Read in PRISM Precipitation Data for the Water Year

```
disp('<a href="matlab: junk=0;">AFReadPrismPrec</a>');
fprintf(1,['\n AFReadPrismPrec: Reading PRISM prec and creating data
structures ',...
    'for %s in %u.\n'],THS,WY);
%
if exist('PIn','var')
    clear PIn
end
%
[GridCodeP,GCAreaSqMi,PIn(:,01),PIn(:,02),PIn(:,03),PIn(:,04),PIn(:,05),PIn(:,
06),...
    PIn(:,07),PIn(:,08),PIn(:,09),PIn(:,10),PIn(:,11),PIn(:,12),PIn(:,13)] =
textread(...
    ['..\HSR',THS(1:2),'00\PRISM\Precipitation\PrismPrecipWY',...
    num2str(WY),'.dat'],repmat(' %f',1,15),'headerlines',4,'delimiter',' ');
%
% Read in GridCodes and ComIDs for the selected hydrologic region
[GridCodeHR,ComIDHR] =
textread(['..\HSR',THS(1:2),'00\Flowlines\GridCodeComID.txt'],...
    '%u%u','headerlines',1,'delimiter',',');
%
```

Intersect GridCodes and ComIDs in Target Hydrologic Subregion

Note: ComID_THS refers to COMIDs in THS where there is a catchment

```
[ComID_THS,ia,ib]    = intersect(ComID_THSFlowLine,ComIDHR);
GridCode_THS         = GridCodeHR(ib);
%
% Pick out GridCodes (catchments) within THS
[GridCodeP_THS,NdxA,NdxB] = intersect(GridCodeP,GridCode_THS);
%
if (length(GridCodeP_THS)==length(GridCode_THS))
    fprintf(1,'  Length of PRISM precipitation and NLCD records match at %u
records.\n',...
        length(GridCodeP_THS));
else
    GridCode_NoMatch = setxor(GridCodeP_THS,GridCode_THS);
    fprintf(1,'  Dropping %u unmatched GridCodes:
\n',length(GridCode_NoMatch));
    for i=1:length(GridCode_NoMatch),
        fprintf(1,'  %u ',GridCode_NoMatch(i));
        % Line feed once every ten lines
        if(i/10==round(i/10))
            fprintf(1,'\n');
        end
    end
    fprintf(1,'\n');
end
%
```

Match Corresponding Records in NLCD and PRISM Precipitation

```
GCAreaSqMi = GCAreaSqMi(NdxA);
PIn        = PIn(NdxA,:);
NLCD11THS = NLCD11THS(NdxB); NLCD12THS = NLCD12THS(NdxB);
NLCD21THS = NLCD21THS(NdxB);
NLCD22THS = NLCD22THS(NdxB); NLCD23THS = NLCD23THS(NdxB);
NLCD31THS = NLCD31THS(NdxB); NLCD32THS = NLCD32THS(NdxB);
NLCD33THS = NLCD33THS(NdxB); NLCD41THS = NLCD41THS(NdxB);
NLCD42THS = NLCD42THS(NdxB); NLCD43THS = NLCD43THS(NdxB);
NLCD51THS = NLCD51THS(NdxB); NLCD61THS = NLCD61THS(NdxB);
NLCD71THS = NLCD71THS(NdxB); NLCD81THS = NLCD81THS(NdxB);
NLCD82THS = NLCD82THS(NdxB); NLCD83THS = NLCD83THS(NdxB);
NLCD84THS = NLCD84THS(NdxB); NLCD85THS = NLCD85THS(NdxB);
NLCD91THS = NLCD91THS(NdxB); NLCD92THS = NLCD92THS(NdxB);
ComID_THS    = ComID_THS(NdxB);
GridCode_THS = GridCode_THS(NdxB);
nTHS         = length(NdxB);
%
%
if ~exist('PrsmPrecTHS','var')
    PrsmPrecTHS = zeros(Ny,nTHS,13);
end
% Store monthly precipitation for time=0 to PIn0
if WY<WY1
    PIn0 = PIn;
else
    PrsmPrecTHS(iy,:,:) = PIn;
end
fprintf(1,' Selected %u records in HSR%s after matching PRISM data.\n',...
    nTHS,THS);
```

Clear Variables

```
clear junk GridCodeHR ComIDHR ia ib
clear GridCodeP GridCode NoMatch NdxA NdxB i
%
```

Appendix 7. Associate NHDPlus Flowlines with Streamflow Gaging Stations (AFGenStrucData)

Contents
- *Setup Structure Variable for Gaging Station Data*
- *Read in Gridcodes and Flowlines Associated Gaging Stations for WY*
- *Clear variables*

Generate structured data file from dbf (csv) file integrating ComIDs and gridcode. The StaTHS info describes gaging stations that have been historically operated in the Target Hydrologic Subregion. Fields in the csv files are: ID, GRIDCODE, OID_, NDX, SUMNO, COMID,

AREASQKM, GRIDCODE_1, FID_1, FID_12, REACHCODE, COMID_1, FROMMEAS, TOMEAS

Explanation for selected fields: GRIDCODE: Unique id for each catchment COMID: Unique id for each reach AREASQKM: Catchment area in square kilometers REACHCODE: 14-digit string identifying HUC.

Setup Structure Variable for Gaging Station Data

```
disp('<a href="matlab: junk=0;">AFGenStrucData</a>');
fprintf(1,'\n                    Creating data structures for all gaging
stations.\n');
fprintf(1,'  Contains GridCode, ComID, AreaSqKm, and ReachCode sets for\n');
fprintf(1,'  historically gaged basins.\n');
%
% Create structure for SubHydrologic Region if doesn't already exist
THSYear = strcat('THS',num2str(WY));
%
% The StationList.txt files contains one field of gaging station numbers
% and as many rows as stations ever gaged in the hydrologic subregion.
Folder   = ['\HSR',THS,'\GagedCatchments\'];
StaTHS   = textread(['..',Folder,'StationList.txt'],'%s');
NStaTHS  = length(StaTHS);   % NStaTHS is the number of gaging stations
%                                 in the Target Hydrologic Subregion
%
% If not existing, initialize matrix to identify which stations...
%   were operating each year during the Period of Analysis (POA)
if ~exist('POA','var');
    POA = zeros(NStaTHS,Ny,'int8');
end
```

Read in Gridcodes and Flowlines Associated Gaging Stations for WY

A separate file is created for each station historically gaged. The file is constructed in ArcMap by use of the Flowtable or VAA navigator. Once the ComID at the gage station is identified, all upstream ComIDs and corresponding catchments (if any) are associated their GridCodes identify all ComIDs and GridCodes upstream of a gaging station.

```
for is=1:NStaTHS,
    [GridCodeWY,ComIDWY,AreaSqKmWY,ReachCodeWY] = textread(...
        ['..',Folder StaTHS{is} '.dat'],...
        '%u %u %f %s','delimiter',',','headerlines',1);
    AFstruct.(HSR)(iy,is).Station     = StaTHS(is);
    AFstruct.(HSR)(iy,is).GridCode    = GridCodeWY;
    AFstruct.(HSR)(iy,is).ComID       = ComIDWY;
    AFstruct.(HSR)(iy,is).AreaSqKm    = AreaSqKmWY;
    AFstruct.(HSR)(iy,is).TotAreaSqMi =
sum(AFstruct.(HSR)(iy,is).AreaSqKm)*...
        0.386102159;
    AFstruct.(HSR)(iy,is).ReachCode   = reshape([ReachCodeWY{:}]',14,[])';
    % The statement below initializes water use but is not used.
    AFstruct.(HSR)(iy,is).WaterUse    = zeros(1,12);
end
```

Clear Variables

```
clear GridCodeWY ComIDWY AreaSqKmWY ReachCodeWY F1 F2 i n
```

Appendix 8. Read in Monthly Streamflow Data at Gaging Stations (AFReadInFlowWY)

Contents
- *Read in monthly flows at gaging stations*
- *Print out flow info*
- *Read in water use data at flowlines*
- *Clear variables*

Read in monthly flows at gaging stations

```
fprintf(1,'\n AFReadInFlowWY: Reading in flows at gaging stations and \n');
fprintf(1,'  water use flows at specified reaches.\n');
% Read in the flow data at active stations for a specific water year
FileIn =
strcat(['..\HSR',THS(1:2),'00\Streamflow\ComIDStationDAMoAnQ'],num2str(WY));
%
[ComIDSta StaWY NWISArea Q(:,01) Q(:,02) Q(:,03) Q(:,04) Q(:,05)...
    Q(:,06) Q(:,07) Q(:,08) Q(:,09) Q(:,10) Q(:,11) Q(:,12) Q(:,13)] =...
    textread([FileIn '.dat'],...
    ['%u %s ',repmat('%f ',1,14)]);
%
% Select gaging stations in the target hydrologic region for the specific
water year
[StaTHSWY, ia, ib] = intersect(StaWY, StaTHS);
Ns = length(ComIDSta);
%
% Flag active gages in network
POA(ib,iy) = 1;
%
```

Print out flow info

```
fprintf(1,['\n  Flows at Gaging Stations in Hydrologic Subregion %s ',...
    'for Water Year %u\n'],THS,WY);
fprintf(1,['  ',repmat('-',1,82),'\n']);
fprintf(1,'   Index  Gaging  Drainage     \n');
fprintf(1,['   Loop  Station  Area (mi2)    Oct       Nov       Dec',...
    '     Jan       Feb       Mar\n']);
fprintf(1,['    THS                         Apr       May       Jun',...
    '     Jul       Aug       Sep\n']);
fprintf(1,['  ',repmat('-',1,82),'\n']);
for is=1:length(ia),
    fprintf(1,['  %3u   %s %7.1f ',repmat('%9.1f ',1,6),'\n'],...
        is,StaWY{ia(is)},NWISArea(ia(is)),Q(ia(is),01),Q(ia(is),02),...
        Q(ia(is),03),Q(ia(is),04),Q(ia(is),05),Q(ia(is),06));
    fprintf(1,['  %3u                        ',repmat('%9.1f ',1,6),'\n'],...
        is,Q(ia(is),07),Q(ia(is),08),Q(ia(is),09),Q(ia(is),10),...
        Q(ia(is),11),Q(ia(is),12));
    if is>1 && isequal(Q(ia(is),:),Q(ia(is-1),:))
        warndlg(['Check for duplicates at station number ',StaWY{ia(is)}],...
            'Duplicate station numbers?');
        return
    end
end
%
```

Read in water use data at flowlines

```
fprintf(1,['  Initializing zero flows in all %u reaches and all ',...
    'months within the THS.\n'],length(PIn));
ReachWU = zeros(length(PIn),12);
% The FileIn needs to modified to utilize water use data for a specific
% water year.
FileIn  = strcat(['..\',HSR,'\WaterUse\ComID WU All']);
[ComID WU wu(:,1) wu(:,2) wu(:,3) wu(:,4) wu(:,5) wu(:,6) wu(:,7) wu(:,8)...
    wu(:,9) wu(:,10) wu(:,11) wu(:,12)] = textread([FileIn '.dat'],...
    ['%u ',repmat('%f ',1,12)]);
%
% Water use data
% Select reaches in THS
[reaches,ai,bi]=intersect(ComID_WU,ComID_THS);
%
fprintf(1,['\n   Water Use in CFS within THS %s (negative indicates ',...
    'withdrawal from reach).\n'],THS);
fprintf(1,['    ',repmat('-',1,82),'\n']);
fprintf(1,['     ComID     Oct   Nov   Dec   Jan   Feb   Mar   Apr ',...
    ' May   Jun   Jul   Aug   Sep\n']);
fprintf(1,['    ',repmat('-',1,82),'\n']);
for i=1:length(ai),
    fprintf(1,['   %8u ',repmat('%6.1f',1,12),'\n'],...
        ComID WU(ai(i)),wu(ai(i),1:12));
end
fprintf(1,['    ',repmat('-',1,82),'\n']);
% Store WU in ReachWU
ReachWU(bi,1:12) = wu(ai,1:12);
```

Clear variables

```
clear i wu ia ib StaTHSWY reaches
```

Appendix 9. Develop and Display Annual Network Design Matrices (AFStaBasinGridComIDWY)

Contents
- *Create station history structure variable*
- *Populate station history*
- *Define the Network Design Matrix*
- *Plot the Network Design Matrix*
- *Printout GridCodes and ComIDs for each subbasin in WY*
- *Clear variables*

```
disp('<a href="matlab: junk=0;">AFStaBasinGridComIDWY</a>');
fprintf(1,'AFStaBasinGridComIDWY: Creating/populating StaHist structure,\n');
fprintf(1,'                       Determining the annual Network Design
Matrix.\n');
% This script generates the network design matrix specific to a given year.
% Station is a list of the historical gaging stations in the current region
% StationQ is a list of all the active gaging stations in a particular year
% StationList is the station numbers active in a given year
% StationNdx is the index within SHR0405.
% global NWISAreaIWY NHDAreaIWY
%
% The intersection below integrates information about gages operated
% historically and gages operated in a specific water year.
```

```
StaList = StationAll(ia); StaList = StationWY(ib);
[StaList,StaNdx,FloNdx]=intersect([AFstruct.(HSR)(iy,:).Station],StaWY);
% Ns is the number of active stations in a given year
Ns = length(StaList);
%
```

Create station history structure variable
```
if ~exist('StaHist','var')
    StaHist = struct('StaList',-9999,'StaNdx',-9999,'NStaAct',-9999,...
        'QTotWY',-9999.,'QAdjWY',-9999.,...
        'QTotIncWY',-9999.,'QAdjIncWY',-9999.);
end
```

Populate station history
```
StaHist(iy).StaList = StaList';
StaHist(iy).StaNdx  = StaNdx';
StaHist(iy).NStaAct = Ns;
%
% QTotWY is the total flow at the gaging stations
QTotWY = Q(FloNdx,:);
% Also, compute the flow adjusted for water use
%
% For each active station in SHR0405, get all the GRIDCODEs
% GridCodes = SHR0405(StationNdx(1)).GridCode;
% For these GridCodes
% NStaAct is the number of active stations in a specific Water Year
for is=1:Ns,
    fprintf(1,'%5u %5u %s \n',is,StaNdx(is),...
        [AFstruct.(HSR)(iy,StaNdx(is)).Station{:}]);
    AFstruct.(HSR)(iy,StaNdx(is)).SBGridCode  = ...
        AFstruct.(HSR)(iy,StaNdx(is)).GridCode;
    AFstruct.(HSR)(iy,StaNdx(is)).SBComID     = ...
        AFstruct.(HSR)(iy,StaNdx(is)).ComID;
    AFstruct.(HSR)(iy,StaNdx(is)).SBAreaSqKm  = ...
        AFstruct.(HSR)(iy,StaNdx(is)).AreaSqKm;
    AFstruct.(HSR)(iy,StaNdx(is)).SBReachCode = ...
        AFstruct.(HSR)(iy,StaNdx(is)).ReachCode;
    [ComIDwu,ia,ib] = intersect(AFstruct.(HSR)(iy,StaNdx(is)).ComID,...
        ComID_WU);
    if ~isempty(ComIDwu)
        fprintf(1,'     Number of reaches with specified WU %u \n',...
            length(ComIDwu));
        [junk,Ndxa,Ndxb] = intersect(ComIDwu,ComID_THS);
        fprintf(1,'ComIDwu= %u, ia = %u, ib = %u\n',ComIDwu,ia,ib);
        AFstruct.(HSR)(iy,StaNdx(is)).WaterUse      = sum(ReachWU(Ndxb,:),1);
    end
end
```

Define the Network Design Matrix

The NetDesign matrix depicts the streamflow gaging station network as a lower diagonal matrix of zeros and ones. The ones along the diagonal represent individual gaging stations in downstream order by station number. Nonzero elements below the diagonal represent basins that are nested within other gaging stations. The NetDesign matrix is used to extract incremental flows (differences between flows measured at upstream and downstream gaging stations) and drainage areas.

Initalize the Network Design Matrix as an identity matrix of the appropriate dimension.

```
NetDesign = eye(Ns);
%
for is=1:(Ns-1),
    % "js" is a local index tracking the station index "is".
    for js=is+1:Ns,
        % Find any common catchments within the two gaging stations
        [GC,Ndx] = intersect(AFstruct.(HSR)(iy,StaNdx(is)).SBGridCode,...
            AFstruct.(HSR)(iy,StaNdx(js)).SBGridCode);
        % If the basins are nested, remove the common catchments from the
        % lower gaged area
        if ~isempty(Ndx)
            NetDesign(js,is) = 1;
            [GC,Ndx] = setxor(AFstruct.(HSR)(iy,StaNdx(js)).SBGridCode,...
                AFstruct.(HSR)(iy,StaNdx(is)).SBGridCode);
            AFstruct.(HSR)(iy,StaNdx(js)).SBGridCode  = ...
                AFstruct.(HSR)(iy,StaNdx(js)).SBGridCode(Ndx);
            AFstruct.(HSR)(iy,StaNdx(js)).SBComID     = ...
                AFstruct.(HSR)(iy,StaNdx(js)).SBComID(Ndx);
            AFstruct.(HSR)(iy,StaNdx(js)).SBAreaSqKm  = ...
                AFstruct.(HSR)(iy,StaNdx(js)).SBAreaSqKm(Ndx);
            AFstruct.(HSR)(iy,StaNdx(js)).SBReachCode = ...
                AFstruct.(HSR)(iy,StaNdx(js)).SBReachCode(Ndx);
        end
    end
end
```

Plot the Network Design Matrix

```
figure(5);
set(gcf(),'Name',['Network Matrix Configuration ' num2str(WY(1))...
    ' for ',THS],'NumberTitle','off');
imagesc(NetDesign,[0,1]); axis square;
title(['Network Matrix Configuration ' num2str(WY(1)) ' for ',THS]);
set(gca,'YTick',1:Ns,'YTickLabel',StaList,'XGrid','On');
ylabel('ORDERED USGS GAGING STAION NUMBER');
xlabel('SEQUENCE NUMBER OF THE ACTIVE GAGING STATION');
colormap([1 1 1;.5 .5 .5]);
% end
%
% Use NetDesign matrix to compute incremental areas at gaged stations
NWISAreaIWY   = NetDesign\NWISArea(FloNdx);
NHDAreaIWY    = NetDesign\[AFstruct.(HSR)(iy,StaNdx).TotAreaSqMi]';
StaHist(iy).NWISAreaIWY = NWISAreaIWY;
StaHist(iy).NHDAreaIWY  = NHDAreaIWY;
%
```

Printout GridCodes and ComIDs for each subbasin in WY

```
fid = fopen(['StaBasinGridComIDWY' num2str(WY) '.dat'],'wt');
% fprintf(1,' WY StaSeq Station SubBasin GridCode  ComID  SBAreaSqMi\n');
for is=1:Ns,
    % find out how many records are in ith station
    Nr = length(AFstruct.(HSR)(iy,StaNdx(is)).SBGridCode);
    for r=1:Nr,
```

```
        %           % Print to file
        fprintf(fid,'%4.0f %3u %s %4u %8u %9u %7.3f \n',...
            WY, is, StaList{is}, r, ...
            AFstruct.(HSR)(iy,StaNdx(is)).SBGridCode(r),...
            AFstruct.(HSR)(iy,StaNdx(is)).SBComID(r),0.3861*...
            AFstruct.(HSR)(iy,StaNdx(is)).SBAreaSqKm(r));
    end
end
fclose(fid);
```

Clear variables

```
clear ComIDwu ia ib junk Ndxa Ndxb fid FileIn i j wu GC Ndx Nj Q
```

Appendix 10. Plot the Relation Between Drainage Areas and Flows at Streamgages (AFPlotAreasFlows)

Contents
- *Plot NHD and NWIS Areas at Gaging Stations*
- *Compute Incremental Areas and Measured and Adjusted Incremental Monthly Flows*
- *Plot the Incremental Areas and Water Yields at Gaging Stations*
- *Clear variables*

Plot NHD and NWIS Areas at Gaging Stations

```
disp('<a href="matlab: junk=0;">AFPlotAreasFlows</a>');
fprintf(1,'AFPlotAreasFlows: Computing Incremental Areas and Flows.\n');
figure(7);
set(gcf(),'Name',['Incremental Areas at Gaging Stations for Water Year ',...
    num2str(WY(1))],'NumberTitle','off');
plot(sqrt(NHDAreaIWY),sqrt(NWISAreaIWY),'r*');
xlabel('NHD  INCREMENTAL AREAS AT GAGES, IN SQRT(SQMI)');
ylabel('NWIS INCREMENTAL AREAS AT GAGES, IN SQRT(SQMI)');
axis equal
axis square
hold on
plot([.1,sqrt(max(max(NHDAreaIWY),max(NWISAreaIWY)))],...
    [.1,sqrt(max(max(NHDAreaIWY),max(NWISAreaIWY)))],'k-');
title(['Incremental Areas at Gaging Stations for Water Year ',...
    num2str(WY(1))]);
hold off
%
```

Compute Incremental Areas and Measured and Adjusted Incremental Monthly Flows

```
QAdjWY = reshape([AFstruct.(HSR)(iy,StaNdx).WaterUse],...
    12,Ns)'     + QTotWY(:,1:12);
QAdjWY(:,13) = mean((reshape([AFstruct.(HSR)(iy,StaNdx).WaterUse],...
    12,Ns)),1)' + QTotWY(:,13);
%
% Compute the incremental flows at gages
QTotIncWY = NetDesign\QTotWY;
QAdjIncWY = NetDesign\QAdjWY;
%
for is=1:Ns,
    AFstruct.(HSR)(iy,StaHist(iy).StaNdx(is)).QMeaTotInc = QTotIncWY(is,:);
    AFstruct.(HSR)(iy,StaHist(iy).StaNdx(is)).QMeaAdjInc = QAdjIncWY(is,:);
end
%
StaHist(iy).QTotWY    = QTotWY;
StaHist(iy).QAdjWY    = QAdjWY;
StaHist(iy).QTotIncWY = QTotIncWY;
StaHist(iy).QAdjIncWY = QAdjIncWY;
%
```

Plot the Incremental Areas and Water Yields at Gaging Stations

```
figure(9);clf('reset');
set(gcf(),'Name',['Incremental Monthly Flows and Incremental Drainage '...
    'NHD Areas at Gaging Stations in WY ' num2str(WY)],...
    'NumberTitle','off','position',figposition);
for im=1:12,
    NdxGE0 = find(QTotIncWY(:,im)>=0);
    h = subplot(4,3,im);
    plot(sqrt(NHDAreaIWY(NdxGE0)),sqrt(QTotIncWY(NdxGE0,im)),'r+');
    hold on
    plot(sqrt(NHDAreaIWY(NdxGE0)),sqrt(QAdjIncWY(NdxGE0,im)),'bo');
    title([MonthName{im},' ',int2str(WY)]);
    if ismember(im,[1,4,7,10])
        ylabel('Sqrt Flow. in ft^3/s');
    end
    if ismember(im,[10,11,12])
        xlabel('Sqrt Drainage Area. in mi^2');
    end
end
```

Clear variables

```
clear h
```

Appendix 11. Plot Image of Monthly Water Yields by Streamgage (AFYieldImage)

Contents

- *AFYieldImage*
- *Compute Measured and Adjusted Incremental Water Yields for Gaged Basins*
- *Plot Incremental Water Yields for Gaged Basins Unadjusted for Water Use*
- *Plot Incremental Water Yields for Gaged Basins Adjusted for Water Use*
- *Clear variables*

AFYieldImage

```
disp('<a href="matlab: junk=0;">AFYieldImage</a>');
fprintf(1,'AFYieldImage: Creating images of water yield.\n');
```

Compute Measured and Ajdusted Incremental Water Yields for Gaged Basins

Compute exact yields in inches from monthly flows in cfs

```
YTotIncWY = QTotIncWY./repmat(NHDAreaIWY,1,13).*...
    repmat((DaysInMo*24*3600*12/5280.^2),length(NHDAreaIWY),1);
YAdjIncWY = QAdjIncWY./repmat(NHDAreaIWY,1,13).*...
    repmat((DaysInMo*24*3600*12/5280.^2),length(NHDAreaIWY),1);
% Store Yields
StaHist(iy).YTotIncWY = YTotIncWY;
StaHist(iy).YAdjIncWY = YAdjIncWY;
%
CLimLo = floor(min(min(YTotIncWY))*10)/10;
CLimHi =  ceil(max(max(YTotIncWY))*10)/10;
%
red = ones(64,1); grn = ones(64,1); blu = ones(64,1);
if CLimLo<0,
    CLimDt          = (CLimHi - CLimLo)/64;
    NStep           = abs(round(CLimLo/CLimDt));
    % Interpolate from red to white
    red(1:NStep)    = ones(NStep,1);
    grn(1:NStep)    = interp1([CLimLo,0],[0,1],linspace(CLimLo,0,NStep));
    blu(1:NStep)    = interp1([CLimLo,0],[0,1],linspace(CLimLo,0,NStep));
    % Interpolate from white to blue
    red(NStep+1:64) = interp1([1,CLimHi],[1,0],linspace(1,CLimHi,64-NStep));
    grn(NStep+1:64) = interp1([1,CLimHi],[1,0],linspace(1,CLimHi,64-NStep));
    blu(NStep+1:64) = ones(64-NStep,1);
else
    % Interpolate from white to blue
    red(1:64)       = linspace(1,0,64);
    grn(1:64)       = linspace(1,0,64);
    blu(1:64)       = ones(64,1);
end
RGB1 = [red grn blu];
%
```

Plot Incremental Water Yields for Gaged Basins Unadjusted for Water Use

```
figure(11);
set(gcf,'Name',['Apparent Incremental Monthly Water Yield in '...
    num2str(WY(1)) ' for ',THS,' Unadjusted for Water Use'],...
    'NumberTitle','off','Colormap',RGB1);
% subplot(1,2,1)
imagesc(YTotIncWY(:,1:12));
set(gca,'XTick',1:12,...
    'XTickLabel',{'Oct','Nov','Dec','Jan','Feb','Mar','Apr','May',...
    'June','July','Aug','Sep'})
set(gca,'YTick',1:Ns,'YTickLabel',StaList);
ylabel('USGS GAGING STATION NUMBER, IN DOWNSTREAM ORDER');
xlabel('MONTH, IN WATER YEAR SEQUENCE');
title(['Apparent Incremental Water Yield Measured in '...
    num2str(WY) ' in inches per month']);
colorbar();
% end
```

```
%
% Flows adjusted for water use
CLimLo = floor(min(min(YAdjIncWY))*10)/10;
CLimHi =  ceil(max(max(YAdjIncWY))*10)/10;
%
red = ones(64,1); grn = ones(64,1); blu = ones(64,1);
if CLimLo<0,
    CLimDt          = (CLimHi - CLimLo)/64;
    NStep           = abs(round(CLimLo/CLimDt));
    % Interpolate from red to white
    red(1:NStep)    = ones(NStep,1);
    grn(1:NStep)    = interp1([CLimLo,0],[0,1],linspace(CLimLo,0,NStep));
    blu(1:NStep)    = interp1([CLimLo,0],[0,1],linspace(CLimLo,0,NStep));
    % Interpolate from white to blue
    red(NStep+1:64) = interp1([1,CLimHi],[1,0],linspace(1,CLimHi,64-NStep));
    grn(NStep+1:64) = interp1([1,CLimHi],[1,0],linspace(1,CLimHi,64-NStep));
    blu(NStep+1:64) = ones(64-NStep,1);
else
    % Interpolate from white to blue
    red(1:64)       = linspace(1,0,64);
    grn(1:64)       = linspace(1,0,64);
    blu(1:64)       = ones(64,1);
end
RGB2 = [red grn blu];
```

Plot Incremental Water Yields for Gaged Basins Adjusted for Water Use

```
figure(12);
set(gcf,'Name',['Apparent Incremental Monthly Water Yield in ',...
    num2str(WY(1)),' for ',THS,' Adjusted for Water Use'],...
    'NumberTitle','off','Colormap',RGB2);
imagesc(YAdjIncWY(:,1:12));
set(gca,'XTick',1:12,...
    'XTickLabel',{'Oct','Nov','Dec','Jan','Feb','Mar','Apr','May',...
    'June','July','Aug','Sep'});
set(gca,'YTick',1:Ns,'YTickLabel',StaList);
title(['Apparent Incremental Water Yield in ' num2str(WY)...
    ' Adjusted for Water Use, in inches per month']);
xlabel('MONTH, IN WATER YEAR SEQUENCE');
ylabel('USGS GAGING STATION NUMBER, IN DOWNSTREAM ORDER');
colorbar();
%
```

Clear Variables

```
clear blu grn red RGB1 RGB2 Nj NStep CLimDT CLimHi CLimLo
```

Appendix 12. Read in PRISM Air Temperature Data (AFReadPrismTemp)

Contents
- *Read in Monthly Average PRISM Temperature*
- *Compute Area-Weighted NLCD Properties for Incremental Gaging Stations*
- *Compute Area-Weighted PRISM Precipitation and Temperature*
- *Clear variables*

Read in Monthly Average PRISM Temperature

stations, store results in HSR file structure TdC represents Temperature in degrees Celsius.

```
disp('<a href="matlab: junk=0;">AFReadPrismTemp</a>');
fprintf(1,'                  Reading Monthly PRISM Temperature Data.\n');
[GridCodeT TdC(:,1) TdC(:,2) TdC(:,3) TdC(:,4) TdC(:,5) TdC(:,6)...
    TdC(:,7) TdC(:,8) TdC(:,9) TdC(:,10) TdC(:,11) TdC(:,12)] = textread(...
    ['..\HSR',THS(1:2),'00\PRISM\Temperature\PrismTempAveWY' num2str(WY)
'.dat'],...
    '%u %f%f%f%f%f%f%f%f%f%f%f%f', 'headerlines',4);
%
% If undefined, allocate array to contain land use info
if ~exist('ArrayNLCD','var')||~exist('PrsmPrec','var')||...
        ~exist('PrsmTemp','var')||~exist('PrsmTempTHS','var');
    ArrayNLCD   =       -ones(Ny,nTHS,21);
    PrsmPrec    = -9999*ones(Ny,nTHS,12);
    PrsmTemp    = -9999*ones(Ny,nTHS,12);
    PrsmTempTHS =        zeros(Ny,nTHS,12);
end
%
[junk,ia,ib]      = intersect(GridCodeP_THS,GridCodeT);
PrsmTempTHS(iy,:,:) = TdC(ib,:);
%
```

Compute Area-Weighted NLCD Properties for Incremental Gaging Stations

```
for is=1:Ns,
    % Find indices of basin
    [set1,ia,ib] = intersect(AFstruct.(HSR)(iy,StaNdx(is)).SBComID,ComID_THS);
    WtLU = repmat(AFstruct.(HSR)(iy,StaNdx(is)).SBAreaSqKm,1,21) .*...
        [NLCD11THS(ib) NLCD12THS(ib) NLCD21THS(ib) NLCD22THS(ib)...
        NLCD23THS(ib) NLCD31THS(ib) NLCD32THS(ib) NLCD33THS(ib)...
        NLCD41THS(ib) NLCD42THS(ib) NLCD43THS(ib) NLCD51THS(ib)...
        NLCD61THS(ib) NLCD71THS(ib) NLCD81THS(ib) NLCD82THS(ib)...
        NLCD83THS(ib) NLCD84THS(ib) NLCD85THS(ib) NLCD91THS(ib)...
        NLCD92THS(ib)];
    %
    AFstruct.(HSR)(iy,StaNdx(is)).NLCD = sum(WtLU)...
        ./ sum(repmat(AFstruct.(HSR)(iy,StaNdx(is)).SBAreaSqKm,1,21));
```

Compute Area-Weighted NLCD Properties for Incremental Gaging Stations

```
for is=1:Ns,
    % Find indices of basin
    [set1,ia,ib] = intersect(AFstruct.(HSR)(iy,StaNdx(is)).SBComID,ComID THS);
    WtLU = repmat(AFstruct.(HSR)(iy,StaNdx(is)).SBAreaSqKm,1,21) .*...
        [NLCD11THS(ib) NLCD12THS(ib) NLCD21THS(ib) NLCD22THS(ib)...
        NLCD23THS(ib) NLCD31THS(ib) NLCD32THS(ib) NLCD33THS(ib)...
        NLCD41THS(ib) NLCD42THS(ib) NLCD43THS(ib) NLCD51THS(ib)...
        NLCD61THS(ib) NLCD71THS(ib) NLCD81THS(ib) NLCD82THS(ib)...
        NLCD83THS(ib) NLCD84THS(ib) NLCD85THS(ib) NLCD91THS(ib)...
        NLCD92THS(ib)];
    %
    AFstruct.(HSR)(iy,StaNdx(is)).NLCD = sum(WtLU)...
        ./ sum(repmat(AFstruct.(HSR)(iy,StaNdx(is)).SBAreaSqKm,1,21));
```

Compute Area-Weighted PRISM Precipitation and Temperature

```
    WtPIn = repmat(AFstruct.(HSR)(iy,StaNdx(is)).SBAreaSqKm,1,12) .*
PIn(ib,1:12);
    % Compute weighted average precip
    AFstruct.(HSR)(iy,StaNdx(is)).Precip = sum(WtPIn)./...
        sum(repmat(AFstruct.(HSR)(iy,StaNdx(is)).SBAreaSqKm,1,12));
    PrsmPrec(iy,StaNdx(is),:) = sum(WtPIn)./...
        sum(repmat(AFstruct.(HSR)(iy,StaNdx(is)).SBAreaSqKm,1,12));
    % Find indices of basin GridCodes
    [set1,ia,ib] =
intersect(AFstruct.(HSR)(iy,StaNdx(is)).SBGridCode,GridCodeT);
    % Compute weighted temperature values in degC
    WtTcD = repmat(AFstruct.(HSR)(iy,StaNdx(is)).SBAreaSqKm,1,12) .*
TdC(ib,1:12);
    % Store weighted average temperature
    AFstruct.(HSR)(iy,StaNdx(is)).Temp = sum(WtTcD)./...
        sum(repmat(AFstruct.(HSR)(iy,StaNdx(is)).SBAreaSqKm,1,12));
    PrsmTemp(iy,StaNdx(is),:) = sum(WtTcD)./...
        sum(repmat(AFstruct.(HSR)(iy,StaNdx(is)).SBAreaSqKm,1,12));
end
%
if (WY == WYn),
    save(['AFstruct.(HSR)_' int2str(WY)],'AFstruct');
end
```

Clear Variables

```
clear CLimDt ia ib set1 WtLU WtPIn WtTcD TdC PIn
```

Appendix 13. Compute the Previous Month's Precipitation (AFGenLag1Precp)

AFGenLag1Precp generates a version of PrsmPrecTHS (PrsmPremTHS) with lag1 (minus) monthly precipitation values.

```
[ii,jj,kk] = size(PrsmPrecTHS);
PrsmPremTHS = zeros(ii,jj,kk-1);
for i=1:ii,
    for j=1:jj,
        for k=1:12,
            if k==1 && i>1
                PrsmPremTHS(i,j,k) = PrsmPrecTHS(i-1,j,12);
            elseif k==1 && i==1
                PrsmPremTHS(i,j,k) = PIn0(j,12);
            else
                PrsmPremTHS(i,j,k) = PrsmPrecTHS(i,j,k-1);
            end
        end
    end
end
clear ii jj kk
```

Appendix 14. Create Boxplots Showing the Distribution of Explanatory Variables (AFBoxplotExplanVar)

Contents

Program that calls AFRegCheckBoxGUI_v1b.m
Specify the number of explanatory variables

```
fprintf(1,'\nBased on the number of explanatory variables specified, a
series\n');
fprintf(1,'of %u screens will be presented to select explanatory
variables\n',Nr);
fprintf(1,'Each screen will correspond to one explanatory variable.\n');
fprintf(1,'Each checked box in the NLCD list will be added to the contents of
\n');
fprintf(1,'the corresponding field to the explanatory variable as a
partial\n');
fprintf(1,'sum.  A checked box in the PRISM climatic variables will be added
as\n');
fprintf(1,'an individual explanatory variable.  The rank of the\n');
fprintf(1,'design matrix will be determined and a boxplot showing the \n');
fprintf(1,'the explanatory variables will be generated as an aid to\n');
fprintf(1,'ensuring that the specified regression equation is
estimatible.\n');
%
```

Read in NLCD Data for the Target Hydrologic Subregion

```
NLCDTHS = [NLCD11THS,NLCD12THS,NLCD21THS,NLCD22THS,NLCD23THS,NLCD31THS,...
    NLCD32THS,NLCD33THS,NLCD41THS,NLCD42THS,NLCD43THS,NLCD51THS,NLCD61THS,...
    NLCD71THS,NLCD81THS,NLCD82THS,NLCD83THS,NLCD84THS,NLCD85THS,NLCD91THS,...
    NLCD92THS];
%
% Initialize the Regression Design Matrix
RegDesignMat = zeros(nTHS,Nr,'single');
%
```

Create Boxplot Showing the Distribution of NLCD Variables

```
figure(20);
boxplot(NLCDTHS,'labels',{'11','12','21','22','23','31','32','33',...
    '41','42','43','51','61','71','81','82','83','84','85','91','92'},...
    'whisker',10000);
xlabel('NATIONAL LAND COVER DATASET (1992) CLASSIFICATION CODE');
ylabel('PERCENTAGE OF CATCHMENT AREA');
set(gcf,'Name','NLCD 1992 Land Use/Cover Data',...
        'NumberTitle','off');
```

Create Boxplot Showing the Distribution of Monthly Precipitation Data

```
figure(21);
boxplot(reshape(PrsmPrecTHS(Ny,:,1:12),[],12),...
    'labels',MoName);
xlabel(['Month of Water Year ',num2str(WY1+Ny-1)]);
ylabel('Precipitation, in inches');
set(gcf,'Name','PRISM Total Monthly Precipitation',...
        'NumberTitle','off');
```

Create Boxplot Showing the Distribution of Monthly Temperature Data

```
figure(22);
boxplot(reshape(PrsmTempTHS(Ny,:,1:12),[],12),...
    'labels',MoName);
xlabel(['Month of Water Year ',num2str(WY1+Ny-1)]);
ylabel('Temperature, in degrees Celcius');
set(gcf,'Name','PRISM Average of Minimum and Maximum Monthly Temperature',...
        'NumberTitle','off');
% Initialize a string array containing the names of the explanatory variables.
```

Appendix 15. Calls Graphical User Interface for User-Specified Water Yield Regression Equation (AFCallRegCheckBox)

Contents

Script to facilitate the selection and retrieval of explanatory variables
Initialize all variable selection indicators to 0.

```
CB11=0; CB12=0; CB21=0; CB22=0; CB23=0; CB31=0; CB32=0; CB33=0; CB41=0;
CB42=0; CB43=0; CB51=0; CB61=0; CB71=0; CB81=0; CB82=0; CB83=0; CB84=0;
CB85=0; CB91=0; CB92=0; CBPT=0; CBTA=0; CBPM=0;

% Run GUI to check off the attributes that are summed to for the
% explanatory variables
%
% Create a default sequential name for each variable.
VarName = ['Var',num2str(ir,'%02u')];
```

Call GUI to Select Explanatory Variables in Regression

```
AFRegCheckBoxGUI v1d

waitfor(gcf)
% Create variable name from default or user specification.
RegVarName{ir} = VarName;
fprintf(1,'Returning from GUI after %2.0f variable named
%s\n',ir,RegVarName{ir});
```

Setup Matrix of Explanatory Variables

CBMatrix (checkbox matrix) contains a 1 for entries checked by the user and a 0 otherwise.

```
CBMatrix(ir,:) = [CB11 CB12 CB21 CB22 CB23 CB31 CB32 CB33 CB41 CB42,...
    CB43 CB51 CB61 CB71 CB81 CB82 CB83 CB84 CB85 CB91 CB92 CBPT CBTA CBPM];
% The first 21 columns of CBMatrix correspond to NLCD attributes
NdxNLCD  = find(CBMatrix(ir,1:21));
```

Identify Explanatory Variables

```
fprintf(1,'Starting test of contents.\n');
if ~isempty(NdxNLCD) && CBPT==0 && CBTA==0
    % If NLCD classes were specified:
    % Sum the columns of the selected NLCD variables to form the explanatory
    % variable.
    RegDesignMat(:,ir) = sum(NLCDTHS(:,NdxNLCD),2);
    %
    % CBPT is the state of the check box for current  monthly precipitation
    % CBPM is the state of the check box for previous monthly precipitation
    % CBTA is the state of the check box for monthly Temperature Average,
    % where the average is computed as the mean of the maximum and minimum.
elseif CBPT==1 && CBTA==0 && isempty(NdxNLCD)
    fprintf(1,'Current monthly precipitation specified.\n');
    RegDesignMat(:,ir) = PrsmPrecTHS(Ny,:,im);
elseif CBPM==1 && CBPT==0 && CBTA==0 && isempty(NdxNLCD)
    fprintf(1,'Previous monthly precipitation specified. \n');
    if Ny == 1 && im == 1;
        RegDesignMat(:,ir) = PInO(:,12)';
    elseif im > 1;
        RegDesignMat(:,ir) = PrsmPrecTHS(Ny,:,im-1)';
```

```
    else Ny > 1 && im ==1;
        RegDesignMat(:,ir) = PrsmPrecTHS(Ny-1,:,12)';
    end
elseif CBPT==0 && CBTA==1 && isempty(NdxNLCD)
    fprintf(1,'Current monthly temperature specified.\n');
    %RegDesignMat(:,ir) = mean(reshape(PrsmTempTHS(Ny,:,1:12),[],12),2);
    RegDesignMat(:,ir) = PrsmTempTHS(Ny,:,im)';
else
    fprintf(1,'\n* * * Improper specification of explanatory variables. * *
*\n');
    errordlg(['No variables selected for the ',num2str(ir),...
        ' explanatory term.'],'No Variables Selected');
    fprintf(1,'STOPPING.\n');
    return
end
```

Plot Distribution of Selected Explanatory Variables

```
figure(23);
boxplot(RegDesignMat(:,1:ir),'labels',RegVarName(1:ir));
xlabel('EXPLANATORY VARIABLES');
ylabel('MAGNITUDE, IN VARIABLES UNITS');
set(gcf,'Name','Distributions of Selected Explanatory Variables',...
        'NumberTitle','off')
%
```

Clear Variables

```
clear CB11 CB12 CB21 CB22 CB23 CB31 CB32 CB33 CB41
clear CB42 CB43 CB51 CB61 CB71 CB81 CB82 CB83 CB84
clear CB85 CB91 CB92 CBPT CBTA CBTH CBTL
```

Appendix 16. Graphical User Interface for User-Specified Regression Equation (AFRegCheckBoxGUI)

GUI for Selection of Regression Equation Variables

```
function AFRegCheckBoxGUI v1c
VarNo = evalin('base','ir');

% Initialize and hide the GUI as it is being constructed.
f = figure('Visible','on','Position',[505,112,741,688],...
    'Color',[.925, .914, .847],'MenuBar','none',...
    'name',...
    'AFINCH: Selection of Explanatory Variables for Regression',...
    'numbertitle','off');

hTitle.Text = uicontrol('Style','text',...
    'Position',[110,637,541,41],'FontSize',14,...
    'FontWeight','demi','HorizontalAlignment','center');
    % VarNo = evalin('ws','VarNo');
    set(hTitle.Text,'String',...
        ['Explanatory Variable ',num2str(VarNo)]);

TopLine.line = annotation('line',[40 690]./741,[630,630]./688);

hSubTitle1.Text = uicontrol('Style','text',...
    'String','NLCD National Land Cover Dataset (1992)',...
    'Position',[150,598,421,25],'FontSize',14,...
    'FontWeight','bold','HorizontalAlignment','center',...
    'ForegroundColor',[0 0 1]);

hWater.Text = uicontrol('Style','text','String','Water','FontSize',12,...
    'FontWeight','bold','ForegroundColor',[0 0 1],...
    'Position',[40,567,51,21],'HorizontalAlignment','left');

OpenWater.CheckBox = uicontrol('Style','checkbox','String','11 Open Water',...
    'FontSize',12,...
    'Position',[40,537,151,29],'HorizontalAlignment','left');

Perennial.CheckBox = uicontrol('Style','checkbox','String','12 Perennial
Ice/Snow',...
    'FontSize',12,...
    'Position',[40,515,190,29],'HorizontalAlignment','left');

Barren.Text = uicontrol('Style','text','String','Barren','FontSize',12,...
    'FontWeight','bold','ForegroundColor',[0,0,1],...
    'Position',[40,477,54,29],'HorizontalAlignment','left');

BareRock.CheckBox = uicontrol('Style','checkbox',...
    'String','31 Bare Rock/Sand/Clay','FontSize',12,...
    'Position',[40,454,211,29],'HorizontalAlignment','left');

Quarries.CheckBox = uicontrol('Style','checkbox','FontSize',12,...
    'String','32 Quarries/Strip Mines/Gravel Pits',...
    'Position',[40,433,284,29],'HorizontalAlignment','left');

Transitional.CheckBox = uicontrol('Style','checkbox','FontSize',12,...
    'String','33 Transitional',...
    'Position',[40,411,141,29],'HorizontalAlignment','left');

ShrubLand.Text =
uicontrol('Style','text','FontSize',12,'FontWeight','bold',...
    'String','Shrubland','ForegroundColor',[0,0,1],...
    'Position',[40,374,141,29],'HorizontalAlignment','left');

Shrubland.CheckBox = uicontrol('Style','checkbox','FontSize',12,...
    'String','51 Shrubland',...
    'Position',[40,352,151,29],'HorizontalAlignment','left');
```

```
Herbaceous.Text =
uicontrol('Style','text','FontSize','12','FontWeight','bold',...
    'String','Herbaceous Upland Natural/Semi-natural
Vegetation','ForegroundColor',[0,0,1],...
    'Position',[40,309,421,26],'HorizontalAlignment','left');

HerbaceousNatural.CheckBox = uicontrol('Style','checkbox','FontSize',12,...
    'String','71 Grasslands/Herbaceous',...
    'Position',[40,289,225,26],'HorizontalAlignment','left');

Wetlands.Text = uicontrol('Style','text','FontSize',12,'FontWeight','bold',...
    'String','Wetlands','ForegroundColor',[0,0,1],...
    'Position',[40,217,91,26],'HorizontalAlignment','left');

Woody.CheckBox = uicontrol('Style','checkbox','FontSize',12,...
    'String','91 Woody Wetlands',...
    'Position',[40,195,173,26],'HorizontalAlignment','left');

Emergent.CheckBox = uicontrol('Style','checkbox','FontSize',12,...
    'String','92 Emergent Herbaceous Wetlands',...
    'Position',[40,173,286,26],'HorizontalAlignment','left');

Developed.Text =
uicontrol('Style','text','FontSize',12,'FontWeight','bold',...
    'String','Developed','ForegroundColor',[0,0,1],...
    'Position',[528,557,161,29],'HorizontalAlignment','right');

LowIntensity.CheckBox = uicontrol('Style','checkbox','FontSize',12,...
    'String','21 Low Intensity Residential',...
    'Position',[480,535,227,26],'HorizontalAlignment','right');

HighIntensity.CheckBox = uicontrol('Style','checkbox','FontSize',12,...
    'String','22 High Intensity Residential',...
    'Position',[476,513,232,26],'HorizontalAlignment','right');

Commercial.CheckBox = uicontrol('Style','checkbox','FontSize',12,...
    'String','23 Commercial/Industrial/Transportation',...
    'Position',[396,491,316,26],'HorizontalAlignment','right');

Forested.Text = uicontrol('Style','text','FontSize',12,'FontWeight','bold',...
    'String','Forested Upland','ForegroundColor',[0,0,1],...
    'Position',[508,442,181,29],'HorizontalAlignment','right');

Deciduous.CheckBox = uicontrol('Style','checkbox','FontSize',12,...
    'String','41 Deciduous Forest',...
    'Position',[526,420,179,29],'HorizontalAlignment','right');

Evergreen.CheckBox = uicontrol('Style','checkbox','FontSize',12,...
    'String','42 Evergreen Forest',...
    'Position',[529,398,177,29],'HorizontalAlignment','right');

Mixed.CheckBox = uicontrol('Style','checkbox','FontSize',12,...
    'String','43 Mixed Forest',...
    'Position',[558,376,145,30],'HorizontalAlignment','right');

NonNatural.Text =
uicontrol('Style','text','FontSize',12,'FontWeight','bold',...
    'String','Non-Natural Woody','ForegroundColor',[0,0,1],...
    'Position',[499,347,191,21],'HorizontalAlignment','right');

Orchards.CheckBox = uicontrol('Style','checkbox','FontSize',12,...
    'String','61 Orchards/Vineyards/Other',...
    'Position',[470,317,238,29],'HorizontalAlignment','right');

HerbaceousPlanted.Text = uicontrol('Style','text','FontSize',12,...
    'FontWeight','bold',...
    'String','Herbaceous Planted/Cultivated','ForegroundColor',[0,0,1],...
    'Position',[443,277,247,29],'HorizontalAlignment','right');
```

```
Pasture.CheckBox = uicontrol('Style','checkbox','FontSize',12,...
    'String','81 Pasture/Hay',...
    'Position',[564,255,139,29],'HorizontalAlignment','right');

RowCrops.CheckBox = uicontrol('Style','checkbox','FontSize',12,...
    'String','82 Row Crops',...
    'Position',[571,233,131,29],'HorizontalAlignment','right');

SmallGrains.CheckBox = uicontrol('Style','checkbox','FontSize',12,...
    'String','83 Small Grains',...
    'Position',[561,211,143,30],'HorizontalAlignment','right');

Fallow.CheckBox = uicontrol('Style','checkbox','FontSize',12,...
    'String','84 Fallow',...
    'Position',[603,189,97,29],'HorizontalAlignment','right');

Urban.CheckBox = uicontrol('Style','checkbox','FontSize',12,...
    'String','85 Urban/Recreational Grasses',...
    'Position',[454,167,261,30],'HorizontalAlignment','right');

hSubTitle2.Text = uicontrol('Style','text',...
    'String','PRISM Monthly Precipitation',...
    'Position',[41,115,331,29],'FontSize',12,...
    'FontWeight','bold','HorizontalAlignment','left',...
    'ForegroundColor',[0 0 1]);

PrecipitationTotal.CheckBox = uicontrol('Style','checkbox','FontSize',12,...
    'String','Concurrent Monthly Total',...
    'Position',[40,90,240,29],'HorizontalAlignment','left');

PrecipitationMinus.CheckBox = uicontrol('Style','checkbox','FontSize',12,...
    'String','Preceding Monthly Total',...
    'Position',[40,65,240,29],'HorizontalAlignment','left');

Temperature.Text =
uicontrol('Style','text','FontSize',12,'FontWeight','bold',...
    'String','PRISM Monthly Temperature','ForegroundColor',[0,0,1],...
    'Position',[390,115,300,29],'HorizontalAlignment','right');

TemperatureAverage.CheckBox = uicontrol('Style','checkbox','FontSize',12,...
    'String','Concurrent Monthly Average',...
    'Position',[474,90,240,29],'HorizontalAlignment','right');

VariableText.Text = uicontrol('Style','text','FontSize',12,...
    'String','Variable name:',...
    'Position',[70,17,151,21],'HorizontalAlignment','right');

VariableEdit.Edit = uicontrol('Style','edit','FontSize',12,...
    'String',['Var',num2str(VarNo,'%02u')],...
    'Position',[230,18,292,21],'HorizontalAlignment','left');

Submit.PushButton = uicontrol('Style','pushbutton','FontSize',12,...
    'String','Submit',...
    'Position',[540,18,70,23],'HorizontalAlignment','center');

MidLine.line = annotation('line',[40 690]./741,[150,150]./688);
```

```
    fprintf(1,'Quarries: %u\n',Quarries.BoxStatus);
end

function Transitional_Callback(gcf, event_data, Transitional)
Transitional.BoxStatus = get(gcf,'Value');
assignin('base','CB33',Transitional.BoxStatus);
fprintf(1,'Transitional: %u\n',Transitional.BoxStatus);
end

function Shrubland_Callback(gcf, event_data, Shrubland)
Shrubland.BoxStatus = get(gcf,'Value');
assignin('base','CB51',Shrubland.BoxStatus);
fprintf(1,'Shrubland: %u\n',Shrubland.BoxStatus);
end

function HerbaceousNatural_Callback(gcf, event_data, HerbaceousNatural)
HerbaceousNatural.BoxStatus = get(gcf,'Value');
assignin('base','CB71',HerbaceousNatural.BoxStatus);
fprintf(1,'HerbaceousNatural: %u\n',HerbaceousNatural.BoxStatus);
end

function Woody_Callback(gcf, event_data, Woody)
Woody.BoxStatus = get(gcf,'Value');
assignin('base','CB91',Woody.BoxStatus);
fprintf(1,'Woody: %u\n',Woody.BoxStatus);
end

function Emergent_Callback(gcf, event_data, Emergent)
Emergent.BoxStatus = get(gcf,'Value');
assignin('base','CB92',Emergent.BoxStatus);
fprintf(1,'Emergent: %u\n',Emergent.BoxStatus);
end

function LowIntensity_Callback(gcf, event_data, LowIntensity)
LowIntensity.BoxStatus = get(gcf,'Value');
assignin('base','CB21',LowIntensity.BoxStatus);
fprintf(1,'LowIntensity: %u\n',LowIntensity.BoxStatus);
end

function HighIntensity_Callback(gcf, event_data, HighIntensity)
HighIntensity.BoxStatus = get(gcf,'Value');
assignin('base','CB22',HighIntensity.BoxStatus);
fprintf(1,'HighIntensity: %u\n',HighIntensity.BoxStatus);
end

function Commercial_Callback(gcf, event_data, Commercial)
Commercial.BoxStatus = get(gcf,'Value');
assignin('base','CB23',Commercial.BoxStatus);
fprintf(1,'Commercial: %u\n',Commercial.BoxStatus);
end

function Deciduous_Callback(gcf, event_data, Deciduous)
Deciduous.BoxStatus = get(gcf,'Value');
assignin('base','CB41',Deciduous.BoxStatus);
fprintf(1,'Deciduous: %u\n',Deciduous.BoxStatus);
end
```

```
function Evergreen Callback(gcf, event data, Evergreen)
Evergreen.BoxStatus = get(gcf,'Value');
assignin('base','CB42',Evergreen.BoxStatus);
fprintf(1,'Evergreen: %u\n',Evergreen.BoxStatus);
end


function Mixed_Callback(gcf, event_data, Mixed)
Mixed.BoxStatus = get(gcf,'Value');
assignin('base','CB43',Mixed.BoxStatus);
fprintf(1,'Mixed: %u\n',Mixed.BoxStatus);
end


function Orchards_Callback(gcf, event_data, Orchards)
Orchards.BoxStatus = get(gcf,'Value');
assignin('base','CB61',Orchards.BoxStatus);
fprintf(1,'Orchards: %u\n',Orchards.BoxStatus);
end


function Pasture Callback(gcf, event data, Pasture)
Pasture.BoxStatus = get(gcf,'Value');
assignin('base','CB81',Pasture.BoxStatus);
fprintf(1,'Pasture: %u\n',Pasture.BoxStatus);
end


function RowCrops Callback(gcf, event data, RowCrops)
RowCrops.BoxStatus = get(gcf,'Value');
assignin('base','CB82',RowCrops.BoxStatus);
fprintf(1,'RowCrops: %u\n',RowCrops.BoxStatus);
end


function SmallGrains Callback(gcf, event data, SmallGrains)
SmallGrains.BoxStatus = get(gcf,'Value');
assignin('base','CB83',SmallGrains.BoxStatus);
fprintf(1,'SmallGrains: %u\n',SmallGrains.BoxStatus);
end


function Fallow Callback(gcf, event data, Fallow)
Fallow.BoxStatus = get(gcf,'Value');
assignin('base','CB84',Fallow.BoxStatus);
fprintf(1,'Fallow: %u\n',Fallow.BoxStatus);
end


function Urban_Callback(gcf, event_data, Urban)
Urban.BoxStatus = get(gcf,'Value');
assignin('base','CB85',Urban.BoxStatus);
fprintf(1,'Urban: %u\n',Urban.BoxStatus);
end


end
function PrecipitationTotal_Callback(gcf, event_data, PrecipitationTotal)
PrecipitationTotal.BoxStatus = get(gcf,'Value');
assignin('base','CBPT',PrecipitationTotal.BoxStatus);
fprintf(1,'PrecipitationTotal: %u\n',PrecipitationTotal.BoxStatus);
end


function PrecipitationMinus Callback(gcf, event data, PrecipitationMinus)
PrecipitationMinus.BoxStatus = get(gcf,'Value');
```

```
assignin('base','CBPM',PrecipitationMinus.BoxStatus);
fprintf(1,'PrecipitationMinus: %u\n',PrecipitationMinus.BoxStatus);
end

function TemperatureAverage Callback(gcf, event data, TemperatureAverage)
TemperatureAverage.BoxStatus = get(gcf,'Value');
assignin('base','CBTA',TemperatureAverage.BoxStatus);
fprintf(1,'TemperatureAverage: %u\n',TemperatureAverage.BoxStatus);
end

function VariableEdit_Callback(gcf, event_data, VariableEdit)
VariableEdit.VarName = get(gcf,'String');
assignin('base','VarName',VariableEdit.VarName);
fprintf(1,'VarName: %s\n',VariableEdit.VarName);
end

function Submit_Callback(gcf, event_data, Submit)
close(gcbf)
end
```

Appendix 17. Estimate Parameters for User-Specified Regression Equation with Data for the Entire Period of Analysis (AFRegressPOA)

Contents

```
AFRegressPOA (Period of Analysis) concatenates all years of data to
identify a set of monthly regression equations that would be appropriate
 if the entire period of analysis were used to estimate the parameters.'
```

Specify the p-value for Entering and Removing Variables

```
dlg title = 'P-value for regression equation:';
prompt = {'P-value for variable enter into regression: ',...
    'P-value for variable removal from regression: '};
    default = {'0.01','0.01'};
Pvalues = inputdlg(prompt,dlg_title,1,default);
Penter  = str2double(Pvalues{1});
Premove = str2double(Pvalues{2});
%
```

Build Concatenated Data Files

Determine the size of the NLCD and climatic components of the regression.

```
NdxNLCD = find(sum(CBMatrix(:, 1:21),2));
NdxPRSM = find(sum(CBMatrix(:,22:24),2));
fprintf(1,['\nThe specified regression contains %u NLCD and %u '...
    'climatic components.\n\n'],...
    length(NdxNLCD),length(NdxPRSM));
%
% Determine the length needed to contain the regression data
nrow = 0;
for iy=1:Ny,
    nrow = nrow + StaHist(iy).NStaAct;
end
%
NRow    = nrow*12;              % Allows for monthly values
NCol    = 4 + Nr;              % Year,Station,Month,YIncAdj,[NLCD],[Climate]
RegMat = zeros(NRow,NCol);
% Initialize row counter nrow
nrow = 0;
```

Build Monthly Regression Matrices

```
for iy=1:Ny,
    WY       = WY1 + iy -1 ;
    NActSta = StaHist(iy).NStaAct;
    for is  = 1:NActSta;
        Station = str2double(StaHist(iy).StaList{is});
        StaNdx  =          StaHist(iy).StaNdx(is);
        for im  = 1:12
            nrow = nrow + 1;
            RegMat(nrow,1) = WY;
            RegMat(nrow,2) = Station;
            % Month of analysis
            RegMat(nrow,3) = im;
            % Incremental water yields adjusted for water use
            RegMat(nrow,4) = StaHist(iy).YAdjIncWY(is,im);
            for ir = 1:Nr,
                if CBMatrix(ir,24) == 1 && im == 1 && iy == 1
                    %prec = zeros(NRow,1);
                    prec =
```

```
AFstruct.(HSR)(iy,StaHist(iy).StaNdx(is)).Precip(im)...
                    * mean(PIn0(:,12))/mean(PrsmPrecTHS(iy,im));
            elseif CBMatrix(ir,24) == 1  && im > 1
                prec =
AFstruct.(HSR)(iy,StaHist(iy).StaNdx(is)).Precip(im-1);
            elseif CBMatrix(ir,24) == 1  && im == 1 && iy > 1
                ndx =
find(strcmp(AFstruct.(HSR)(iy,StaHist(iy).StaNdx(is)).Station,...
                [AFstruct.(HSR)(iy-1,StaHist(iy-1).StaNdx).Station]));
            if ~isempty(ndx)
                prec = AFstruct.(HSR)(iy-1,StaHist(iy-
1).StaNdx(ndx)).Precip(12);
            else
                prec = mean(PrsmPrecTHS(iy-1,:,12));
            end
        else
            prec = 0;
        end
        RegMat(nrow,4+ir) = CBMatrix(ir,1:21) * ...
            AFstruct.(HSR)(iy,StaHist(iy).StaNdx(is)).NLCD' + ...
CBMatrix(ir,22)*AFstruct.(HSR)(iy,StaHist(iy).StaNdx(is)).Precip(im)+...
CBMatrix(ir,23)*AFstruct.(HSR)(iy,StaHist(iy).StaNdx(is)).Temp(im)+...
            CBMatrix(ir,24)*prec;
            % Compute column of previous month precipitation
        end
        end
    end
end
%
```

Stepwise Regression Analysis for Monthly Water Yield

```
RegMonth = struct([]);
for im=1:12,
    Ndx = find(RegMat(:,3)==im);
    [RegMonth(im).b,RegMonth(im).se,RegMonth(im).pval,RegMonth(im).inmodel, ...
        RegMonth(im).stats ] = stepwisefit(RegMat(Ndx,5:4+ir), ...
        RegMat(Ndx,4),'penter',Penter,'premove',Premove);
end
%
% Define R2B as a matrix where negative values are red, 0 values are white,
% and positive values are blue.
R2B = [[ones(32,1);linspace(1,0,32)'],...
        [linspace(0,1,32)'; linspace(1,0,32)'],...
        [linspace(0,1,32)'; ones(32,1)]];
%
```

Plot Image of Monthly Regression Variable Significance

```
figure(58);
% Create figure color coding the significant variables by month.
% Red areas show significant negative coefficients, blue areas show
% significant positive coefficients, and white areas show no significant
% coefficients.

imagesc([RegMonth(01).inmodel'.* RegMonth(01).b ./ RegMonth(01).se, ...
        RegMonth(02).inmodel'.* RegMonth(02).b ./ RegMonth(02).se, ...
        RegMonth(03).inmodel'.* RegMonth(03).b ./ RegMonth(03).se, ...
        RegMonth(04).inmodel'.* RegMonth(04).b ./ RegMonth(04).se, ...
        RegMonth(05).inmodel'.* RegMonth(05).b ./ RegMonth(05).se, ...
        RegMonth(06).inmodel'.* RegMonth(06).b ./ RegMonth(06).se, ...
        RegMonth(07).inmodel'.* RegMonth(07).b ./ RegMonth(07).se, ...
        RegMonth(08).inmodel'.* RegMonth(08).b ./ RegMonth(08).se, ...
        RegMonth(09).inmodel'.* RegMonth(09).b ./ RegMonth(09).se, ...
        RegMonth(10).inmodel'.* RegMonth(10).b ./ RegMonth(10).se, ...
        RegMonth(11).inmodel'.* RegMonth(11).b ./ RegMonth(11).se, ...
        RegMonth(12).inmodel'.* RegMonth(12).b ./ RegMonth(12).se],[-10.10]);
%
```

```
colormap(R2B)
colorbar('location','SouthOutside');
set(gca,'YTick',1:6,...
    'YTickLabel',RegVarName,'XTick',1:12,...
    'XTickLabel',MoName);
set(gcf,'NumberTitle','Off','Name',...
['Monthly t-values for Significant (p<=',...
num2str(max(Penter,Premove),3),') Parameters across all Years']);
title(['Monthly t-values for Significant (p<=',...
    num2str(max(Penter,Premove),3),') Parameters for the period of
analysis.']);
%
% Print out model statistics for each month
ndash = 63;
fprintf(1,'Monthly Regression Results for Period of Analysis \n');
fprintf(1,['',repmat('-',1,ndash),'\n']);
fprintf(1,'         Number of   Degrees                          \n');
fprintf(1,'         explanatory   of                             \n');
fprintf(1,'Month   variables   Freedom   RMSE    F-stat    p-value    r2 \n');
fprintf(1,['',repmat('-',1,ndash),'\n']);
for im=1:12,
    fprintf(1,'%5s       %u       %u %9.4f %8.2f %10.5f    %6.4f\n',...
    MoName{im},...
    RegMonth(1,im).stats.df0,...
    RegMonth(1,im).stats.dfe,...
    RegMonth(1,im).stats.rmse,...
    RegMonth(1,im).stats.fstat,...
    RegMonth(1,im).stats.pval,...
    1-RegMonth(1,im).stats.SSresid/RegMonth(1,im).stats.SStotal);
end
fprintf(1,['',repmat('-',1,ndash),'\n']);
```

Clear Variables

```
clear dlg_title default prompt Penter Premove Pvalues ndash
```

Appendix 18. Estimate Parameters for Regression Equation by Water Year (AFRegressByWY)

Contents

- *Compute Ordinarly Least-Squares and Robust Estimates of Parameters*
- *Plot Ordinary Least-Squares and Robust Estimates of Parameters*
- *Clear Variables*

Develop monthly models by water year RegHist = struct([]); for iy=1:Ny,

```
global iy
WY = WY1 + iy -1;
% fprintf(1,'WY= %u, iy= %u\n',WY,iy);
```

Compute Ordinarly Least-Squares and Robust Estimates of Parameters

```
NdxWY = find(RegMat(:,1)==WY);
for im=1:12,
    NdxMo  = find(RegMat(:,3)==im);
    % NdxObs: Index of observations in WY and im
    NdxObs = intersect(NdxWY,NdxMo);
    NdxXvar  = find(RegMonth(im).inmodel);
    RegDesign = RegMat(NdxObs,4+NdxXvar);
    %
    % Compute Robust Regression Coefficients
    [RegHist(iy,im).RobustB,RegHist(iy,im).RobustStats] = ...
        robustfit(RegDesign,RegMat(NdxObs,4),'fair');
    % Add column of ones for OLS regression
    RegDesignAug = [ones(length(RegDesign),1) RegDesign];
    RegHist(iy,im).RobustPredRUAdj  = (RegDesignAug *
[RegHist(iy,im).RobustB]);
    % Compute OLS Regression Coefficients
    [RegHist(iy,im).b,RegHist(iy,im).bint,RegHist(iy,im).r,...
        RegHist(iy,im).rint,RegHist(iy,im).stats] = ...
        regress(RegMat(NdxObs,4),RegDesignAug);
    RegHist(iy,im).OLSPredRUAdj = (RegDesignAug * RegHist(iy,im).b);
    %
    %if ismember(iy+WY0,ShowWY)
```

Plot Ordinary Least-Squares and Robust Estimates of Parameters

```
    figure(60);
    h = subplot(4,3,im);
    plot(RegMat(NdxObs,4),RegHist(iy,im).RobustPredRUAdj,'r+');
    hold on
    h=plot(RegMat(NdxObs,4),RegHist(iy,im).OLSPredRUAdj,'bo');
    title([MonthName{im},' ', int2str(WY)]);
    if ismember(im,[10,11,12])
        xlabel('Measured Water Yield');
    end
    if ismember(im,[1,4,7,10]);
        ylabel('Estimated Water Yield');
    end
    RobR = corrcoef(RegMat(NdxObs,4),RegHist(iy,im).RobustPredRUAdj);
    YLim = get(gca,'YLim'); YLoLim = YLim(1)+.10*(YLim(2)-YLim(1));
    XLim = get(gca,'XLim'); XUpLim = XLim(2)-.22*(XLim(2)-XLim(1));
    line([XLim(1)+.1 XLim(2)-.1],[XLim(1)+.1 XLim(2)-.1],'Color','k');
    text(XUpLim,YLoLim,['r P^{2}= ',...
        num2str(RobR(1,2)^2,'%6.4f')],'FontSize',8,'Color','r');
    %end
    hold off
end
set(gcf,'Name',['Measured and Estimated Incremental Water Yields at Gaging
Stations in WY ',...
    num2str(WY) ' (red pluses are robust estimates, blue circles are OLS
estimates).'],...
    'NumberTitle','off','position',figposition);
```

Clear Variables

```
clear h
```

Appendix 19. Plot Annual Estimates of Regression Equation Parameters (AFPlotRegressCoeff)

Contents

- *Plot Regression Coefficients by Month*

Plot regression coefficients by month for period of record
Plot Regression Coefficients by Month

Create a figure window

```
figure(82); clf(82);
% Determine how many parameters there are for a particular month
% ID the figure
set(gcf,'NumberTitle','Off','Name',...
    ['Period of Record Regression Coefficients for ',MonthName{im},...
    ' in Target Hydrologic Subregion ', HSR],'position',figposition);
NPar    = 1+ sum([RegMonth(im).inmodel]);
% Determine which parameters are significant in the POA models
NdxPar = find([RegMonth(im).inmodel]);
%
% Dump the regression coefficients for each month during the POA
BetaMatrix = [RegHist(:,im).b];
BetaRobust = [RegHist(:,im).RobustB];
BIntMatrix = [RegHist(:,im).bint]';
% NrMo: Number of regression variables in the ir-th month
NrMo = size(BetaMatrix,1);
% Build subplots for intercept and each parameter
for ir=1:NrMo,
    subplot(NrMo,1,ir);
    set(gca,'XTick',0:5:(Ny+5),...
        'XTickLabel',(WY1-1):5:(WYn+5),...
        'xlim',[0,Ny+1]);
    hold on
    plot(BetaMatrix(ir,:),'bo');
    ylabel({'PARAMETER','ESTIMATE'});
    plot(BetaRobust(ir,:),'rx');
    if ir == 1, VarName = {'Intercept'};
    else
        VarName = RegVarName(NdxPar(ir-1));
        % Display zero reference
        plot([1,Ny],[0 0],'k--');
        % Display Month reference
        plot([1,Ny],[RegMonth(im).b(NdxPar(ir-1))  ...
            RegMonth(im).b(NdxPar(ir-1))],'g-');
        % Plot confidence interval
        for l=1:Ny
            line([l,l],[BIntMatrix(2*l-1,ir),...
                BIntMatrix(2*l,ir)],'Color','b');
        end
    end
    if ir == NrMo
        xlabel('YEAR');
    end
    title(VarName{:});
end
%
```

Appendix 20. Compute Estimates of Adjusted Incremental Water Yields and Flows (AFQEstAdjInc)

Compute estimates of adjusted incremental water yields and flows

```
global iy
WY = WY1 + iy  -1;
%
NdxWY  = find(RegMat(:,1)==WY);
for im=1:12,
    for ir=1:Nr,
        for ir = 1:Nr,
            RegDesign(:,ir) = NLCDTHS  * CBMatrix(ir,1:21)' + ...
                PrsmPrecTHS(iy,:,im)' .* CBMatrix(ir,22)   + ...
                PrsmTempTHS(iy,:,im)' .* CBMatrix(ir,23)   + ...
                PrsmPremTHS(iy,:,im)' .* CBMatrix(ir,24);
        end
    end
    % Update explanatory variables for specific month
    NdxReg     = find(RegMonth(im).inmodel);
    % Update design matrix for month
    RegDesign  = RegDesign(:,NdxReg);
    YEstAdjInc(iy,:,im) = [ones(length(RegDesign),1) RegDesign]*...
        [RegHist(iy,im).RobustB];
    QEstAdjInc(iy,:,im) = YEstAdjInc(iy,:,im)' .* GCAreaSqMi ...
        * 5280^2 /(DaysInMo(im)*24*3600*12);
end
```

Appendix 21. Compute Constrained Estimates of Adjusted Incremental Water Yields and Flows (AFQConAdjInc)

Compute Constrained Estimates of Adjusted Incremental Flows and Yields

```
global iy
%
for is=1:length(StaHist(iy).StaNdx)
    % The target below is ib, the indices for the selected station
    [junk,ia,ib] = intersect(...
        [AFstruct.(HSR)(iy,StaHist(iy).StaNdx(is)).SBGridCode],...
        GridCode_THS);
    % Sum the estimated flows in all catchments for each station by
    % year and month
    AFstruct.(HSR)(iy,StaHist(iy).StaNdx(is)).QEstAdjInc = ...
        reshape(sum(QEstAdjInc(iy,ib,:),2),1,12);
    for im = 1:12,
        ConAdjust(iy,is,im) = ...
            AFstruct.(HSR)(iy,StaHist(iy).StaNdx(is)).QMeaAdjInc(im)/...
            AFstruct.(HSR)(iy,StaHist(iy).StaNdx(is)).QEstAdjInc(im);
        QConAdjInc(iy,ib,im) =  ConAdjust(iy,is,im)*QEstAdjInc(iy,ib,im);
        YConAdjInc(iy,ib,im) = QConAdjInc(iy,ib,im)'./GCAreaSqMi(ib)/...
            ((5280^2)/(DaysInMo(im)*24*3600*12));
    end
end
```

Appendix 22. Plot Monthly Estimates of Flows for the Period of Analysis (AFPlotQmMeaEst)

Plot Monthly Measured and Estimated Flows

```
global iy
WY = WY + 1;
QEstAdjInciy =
reshape([AFstruct.(HSR)(iy,StaHist(iy).StaNdx).QEstAdjInc]',12,[])';
QMeaAdjInciy =
reshape([AFstruct.(HSR)(iy,StaHist(iy).StaNdx).QMeaAdjInc]',13,[])';
%
if ~exist('SRho','var')
    SRho = zeros(Ny,12);
end
%
figure(200);
clf(200);
set(gcf,'NumberTitle','Off','Name',...
    ['Relation between the measured and estimated monthly adjusted ',...
    'incremental flows for WY ',int2str(WY)]);
for im=1:12,
    subplot(4,3,im);
    NdxGT0 = find(QMeaAdjInciy(:,im)>=0 & QEstAdjInciy(:,im)>=0);
    if length(QMeaAdjInciy(:,im))-length(NdxGT0)>0
        fprintf(1,['For WY= %u, iy= %u, and im= %u there are %u ',...
            'positive indices and %u negative indices.\n'],...
            WY,iy,im,length(NdxGT0),length(QMeaAdjInciy(:,im))-
length(NdxGT0));
    end
    plot(sqrt(QMeaAdjInciy(NdxGT0,im)),sqrt(QEstAdjInciy(NdxGT0,im)),'rx');
    title([MonthName{im},' ',num2str(WY)]);
    SRho(iy,im) = corr(QMeaAdjInciy(NdxGT0,im),QEstAdjInciy(NdxGT0,im),...
        'type','Spearman');
    YLim = get(gca,'YLim'); YLoLim = YLim(1)+.10*(YLim(2)-YLim(1));
    XLim = get(gca,'XLim'); XUpLim = XLim(2)-.22*(XLim(2)-XLim(1));
    line([XLim(1)+1 XLim(2)-1],[XLim(1)+1 XLim(2)-1],'Color','k');
    text(XUpLim*.95,YLoLim*1.05,['r_S^{2}= ',...
        num2str(SRho(iy,im)^2,'%6.4f')],'FontSize',8,'Color','r');
    if ismember(im,7)
        ylabel({'SQUARE ROOT OF ESTIMATED FLOW, IN CUBIC FEET PER SECOND'});
    end
    if ismember(im,[10,11,12])
        xlabel({'SQUARE ROOT OF MEASURED','FLOW, IN CUBIC FEET PER SECOND'});
    end
end
```

Appendix 23. Write Estimates of Water Yields and Flows to Files (AFWrtQYEstCon)

Contents
- *Write Constrained and unconstrained estimates of flow and water yield*

Write Constrained and unconstrainted estimates of flow and water yield

```
global iy
WY = WY + 1;
%
fid =
fopen(['..\',HSR,'\Output\FlowYield\QY',HSR,'WY',int2str(WY),'.csv'],'wt');
fprintf(1,'Saving QYHSR%sWY%u.csv\n',THS,WY);
fprintf(fid,'GridCode,ComID,AreaSqMi,');
fprintf(fid,'QEstAdjOct,QEstAdjNov,QEstAdjDec,QEstAdjJan,');
fprintf(fid,'QEstAdjFeb,QEstAdjMar,QEstAdjApr,QEstAdjMay,');
fprintf(fid,'QEstAdjJun,QEstAdjJul,QEstAdjAug,QEstAdjSep,');
fprintf(fid,'YEstAdjOct,YEstAdjNov,YEstAdjDec,YEstAdjJan,');
fprintf(fid,'YEstAdjFeb,YEstAdjMar,YEstAdjApr,YEstAdjMay,');
fprintf(fid,'YEstAdjJun,YEstAdjJul,YEstAdjAug,YEstAdjSep,');
fprintf(fid,'QConAdjOct,QConAdjNov,QConAdjDec,QConAdjJan,');
fprintf(fid,'QConAdjFeb,QConAdjMar,QConAdjApr,QConAdjMay,');
fprintf(fid,'QConAdjJun,QConAdjJul,QConAdjAug,QConAdjSep,');
fprintf(fid,'YConAdjOct,YConAdjNov,YConAdjDec,YConAdjJan,');
fprintf(fid,'YConAdjFeb,YConAdjMar,YConAdjApr,YConAdjMay,');
fprintf(fid,'YConAdjJun,YConAdjJul,YConAdjAug,YConAdjSep\n');
for iTHS=1:nTHS,
    fprintf(fid,['%u,%u,',repmat('%f,',1,48),'%f\n'],...

GridCode THS(iTHS),ComID THS(iTHS),GCAreaSqMi(iTHS),QEstAdjInc(iy,iTHS,1:12),
..

YEstAdjInc(iy,iTHS,1:12),QConAdjInc(iy,iTHS,1:12),YConAdjInc(iy,iTHS,1:12));
end
fclose(fid);
%
% If this is the last year of the analysis, write out the activity status
if iy == Ny
    fprintf(1,'Writing station activity matrix (StationPOA.csv) for period of
analysis.\n');
    % Site,WY[1],WY[2],...WY[Ny]
    fid = fopen(['..\',HSR,'\Output\FlowYield\StationPOA.csv'],'wt');
    fprintf(fid,['Site',repmat(',WY%u',1,Ny),'\n'],WY1-1+[1:Ny]);
    for is=1:Ns,
        fprintf(fid,['"%s"',repmat(',%u',1,Ny),'\n'],StaTHS{is},POA(is,:));
    end
    fclose(fid);
end
```

Appendix 24. Accumulate Flows Throughout the NHDPlus Network (AFConFlowAccum)

Contents
- *Accumulate Flow Using the Algorithm in the NHDPlus User Guide*
- *Accumulate Monthly Flows*
- *Plot Constrained Cumulative and Measured Monthly Flows by Month*
- *Write Constrained Flows*

Accumulate Flow Using the Algorithm in the NHDPlus User Guide

Algorithm shown on p. 47 in the user guide. Read in the HSR VAA table Columns in X: ComID, FromNode, ToNode, HydroSeq, Divergence, Startflag

```
X = csvread(['..\',HSR,'\GIS\NHDFlowlineVAA.txt'],1);

Nx = length(X);
% Sort matix on ComID
X          = sortrows(X,1);
ComIDVAA   = X(:,1);
% %%
% Initialize the FlowAccum Matrix
FlowAccum = zeros(Nx,12);
% Read in monthly incremental flows and water yields in catchments
% GridCode,ComID,DAreaSqMi,QEstAdjOct,QEstAdjNov,...,YConAdjSep
Y = csvread(['..\',HSR,'\Output\FlowYield\QY',HSR,...
    'WY',int2str(WY1+iy-1),'.csv'],1);
%
% MODIFY THE FOLLOWING LINE TO READ IN ANNUALLY VARYING WATER USE DATA
[WUComID,WU(:,1),WU(:,2),WU(:,3),WU(:,4),WU(:,5),WU(:,6),WU(:,7),...
    WU(:,8),WU(:,9),WU(:,10),WU(:,11),WU(:,12)] = ...
    textread(['..\',HSR,'\WaterUse\ComID WU All.dat'],...
    '%u%f%f%f%f%f%f%f%f%f%f%f%f','delimiter','\t');
```

Accumulate Monthly Flows

```
for im=1:12,
    % Find all the common ComIDs
    ComIDVAA            = X(:,1);
    [ComIDCom,ia,ib]    = intersect(ComIDVAA,Y(:,2));
    IncreFlow           = zeros(Nx,1);
    % Reading in the constrained adjusted incremental flows at catchments
    % for each month, which were previously computed.
    IncreFlow(ia)       = Y((ib),27+im);
```

Sort on Hydroseq in decending order

```
    Xaug        = sortrows([X IncreFlow],-4);
    % Partition sorted information
    ComIDVAA    = Xaug(:,1);
    FromNode    = Xaug(:,2);
    ToNode      = Xaug(:,3);
    HydroSeq    = Xaug(:,4);
    Divergence  = Xaug(:,5);
    StartFlag   = Xaug(:,6);
    GridCodeVAA = Xaug(:,7);
    DAreaSqMi   = Xaug(:,8) * 0.386102;
    IncreFlow   = Xaug(:,9);
    %
    % Start accumulating flow
    % Re-initialize FlowAccum with monthly water use data
    for iw=1:length(WUComID),
        NdxWU = find(WUComID(iw)==ComIDVAA);
        % Put withdrawals back into the stream
        FlowAccum(NdxWU,im) = -WU(iw,im);
    end
    %
    % Vector to flag areas that have already been accounted for.
    for ix=1:Nx,
        if HydroSeq(ix)>0,
            if StartFlag(ix)==1 || Divergence(ix)==2
                FlowAccum(ix,im)  =  IncreFlow(ix);
                Ndx = 1;
            else
                Ndx = find(ToNode==FromNode(ix));
                FlowAccum(ix,im)  = sum(FlowAccum(Ndx,im)) + IncreFlow(ix);
            end
        end
    end
    %
```

Read in Station and ComID pairs

```
[HRStation,HRComID] = textread(['..\',HSR(1:5),...
    '00\Flowlines\StationComID.csv'],'%s%u',...
    'headerlines',1,'delimiter',',');

HRStaNum = zeros(length(HRStation),1);
for ig = 1:length(HRStation),
    HRStaNum(ig) = str2double(HRStation{ig});
end
%
AccStaFlow = zeros(length(StaHist(iy).StaList),1);
for is=1:length(StaHist(iy).StaList)
    Ndx = find(str2double(StaHist(iy).StaList{is})==HRStaNum);
    ComIDTarget = HRComID(Ndx);
    % Find the Ndx of the ComIDTarget in the dataset
    ComIDNdx       = find(ComIDTarget==ComIDVAA);
    AccStaFlow(is) = FlowAccum(ComIDNdx,im);
    % Find the measured monthly flows in StaHist(ii).StaList(i)
    fprintf(1,' %4u %4u %4s  %s %4u   %10u %7.1f %7.1f\n',is,...
        WY1+iy-1,MonthName{im}(1:3),StaHist(iy).StaList{is},...
        Ndx,ComIDTarget,AccStaFlow(is),StaHist(iy).QTotWY(is,im));
end
QTotAdj = StaHist(iy).QTotWY;
%
```

Plot Constrained Cumulative and Measured Monthly Flows by Month

```
%    % This code was helpful in debugging but slows processing
%    figure(17);
%    set(gcf,'NumberTitle','off','Name',['Relation between Constrained
Cumulative ',...
%        'and Measured Monthly Flows for USGS Gaging Stations Operated in
',...
%        HSR,' during WY',int2str(WY1+iy-1)]);
%    %
%    subplot(4,3,im)
%    loglog(QTotAdj(:,im),AccStaFlow,'r*');
%    axis([ 1 10^ceil(max(log10(QTotAdj(:,im)))) 1
10^ceil(max(log10(AccStaFlow)))]);
%    title([MonthName{im},' ',int2str(WY1+iy-
1)],'FontWeight','bold','FontSize',10);
%    if ismember(im,[1,4,7,10]),
%        ylabel('Accumulated Flow, ft3/s');
%    end
%    if ismember(im,[10,11,12]),
%        xlabel('Measured Flow, ft3/s');
%    end
%    Ylim = get(gca,'YLim'); Xlim = get(gca,'XLim');
%    line([Xlim(1)*1.1,Xlim(2)*0.9],[Xlim(1)*1.1,Xlim(2)*0.9]);
%    %
end
```

Write Constrained Flows

```
fprintf(1,'Writing output file: %s\n',...
    ['..\',HSR,'\Output\FlowAccum\ComIDQ12WY',int2str(WY1+iy-1),'.csv']);
fid = fopen(['..\',HSR,'\Output\FlowAccum\ComIDQ12WY',...
    int2str(WY1+iy-1),'.csv'],'wt');
% Note: FlowAccums are total constrained flows where water use has been
% accounted for through the network (unadjusted).
fprintf(fid,'ComIDVAA,QAccConOct,QAccConNov,QAccConDec,QAccConJan,QAccConFeb,'
);
fprintf(fid,['QAccConMar,QAccConApr,QAccConMay,QAccConJun,QAccConJul,',...
    'QAccConAug,QAccConSep\n']);
for ix=1:Nx,
    fprintf(fid,['%u',repmat(',%f',1,12),'\n'],...
        ComIDVAA(ix),FlowAccum(ix,1:12));
end
fclose(fid);
```

Appendix 25. Plot Time Series of Monthly Flows and Display Monthly Flow Duration Curves (AFTrendDurations)

Contents

```
 This script computes and plots a flow-duration graph for a specified
 ComID using the constrained accumulated monthly flow estimates
```
FDC is initialized to contain monthly flow-duration data
```
FDC = zeros(Ny,12);
FlagStation = 0;
```
Read in Cumulative Flow Information
```
if ~exist('TrendDurationMatrix','var')
    TrendDurationMatrix = struct([]);
    for iy=1:Ny,
        TrendDurationMatrix(iy).ComIDQm = csvread(...
            ['..\',HSR,'\Output\FlowAccum\ComIDQ12WY',...
            int2str(WY1+iy-1),'.csv'],1);
    end
    alpha = 0.025; a1 = 0.10; g1 = 0.10;
end
% Request the alpha level for the trend test and smoothing parameters.
a = inputdlg({'Alpha level for trend test (0.025)',...
    'Smoothing Constant Parameter a1 (0.10)',...
    'Smoothing Trend Parameter g1 (0.10)'},...
    'Trend and Smoothing Parameters',[1 1 1],...
    {num2str(alpha),num2str(a1),num2str(g1)});
% Update trend and smoothing parameters
alpha = str2double(a{1});
a1    = str2double(a{2});
g1    = str2double(a{3});
method = questdlg('Method for describing temporal variations in flow? ',...
    'Select Descriptor','Linear','Moving Average','Moving Average');
%
% ComIDTarget is the targeted flowline returned from the AFinch GUI.
for iy=1:Ny,
    ComIDNdx = find(TrendDurationMatrix(iy).ComIDQm(:,1)==ComIDTarget);
    if ~isempty(ComIDNdx),
        FDC(iy,1:12) = TrendDurationMatrix(iy).ComIDQm(ComIDNdx,2:13);
        fprintf(1,'Reading accumulated monthly flows for WY%4u. \n',WY1+iy-1);
    else
        fprintf(1,'Requested ComID %u was not found. Stopping.\n',...
            ComIDTarget);
        errordlg('Target ComID not found.  Terminating analysis.',...
            'ComID Not found.')
        return
    end
end
%
```

```
% Determine if there is a gaging station at the targeted flowline.
NdxComID = find(ComIDTarget==HRComID);
Qm = zeros(Ny,13);
if ~isempty(NdxComID)
    % Use the first, because the flowline flows are the same.
    NdxComID = NdxComID(1);
    StationTarget = ['0',num2str(HRStaNum(NdxComID))];
    for iy=1:Ny,
        % Find the index of the station for the current year
        NdxStation = find(strcmp(StaHist(iy).StaList,StationTarget));
        % If the station was operated in the current year, retrieve flows
        if ~isempty(NdxStation)
            % Flag indicating station active in at least one year
            FlagStation = 1;
            % Store measured monthly flows in Qm matrix
            Qm(iy,1:12) = StaHist(iy).QTotWY(NdxStation,1:12);
            % Indicate that flow was measured for that station year
            Qm(iy,13) = 1;
        end
    end
else
    NdxStation = []; stationTarget = [];
end
%
% Find indices of measured monthly flows
NdxMea = find(Qm(:,13)==1);
if ~isempty(NdxMea)
    FDCM    = Qm(NdxMea,1:12);
    [rowFDCM,colFDCM] = size(FDCM);
end
fprintf(1,'Finished reading monthly flow data.\n\n');
%
```

Compute Flow Duration by Month and Plot Curve

```
figure(20); clf(20);
% The if-else-end statement titles the plot differently depending on whether
% or not a streamflow gaging station were operated on the target ComID.
if FlagStation==1
    set(gcf,'NumberTitle','off','Name',['Monthly Flow Duration Curves for
',...
        'ComID ',int2str(ComIDTarget),' in ',HSR,' at gaging station ',...
        StationTarget,' based on AFinch data from WY',...
        int2str(WY1),' to WY',int2str(WY1+Ny-1)],...
        'MenuBar','none','ToolBar','Figure');
    FigLabel = ['Monthly Flow Duration Curves for ',...
        'ComID ',int2str(ComIDTarget),' in ',HSR,' at gaging station ',...
        StationTarget,' from WY',...
        int2str(WY1),' to WY',int2str(WY1+Ny-1)];
else
    set(gcf,'NumberTitle','off','Name',['Monthly Flow Duration Curves for
',...
        'ComID ',int2str(ComIDTarget),' in ',HSR,...
        ' based on AFinch data from WY',...
        int2str(WY1),' to WY',int2str(WY1+Ny-1)],...
        'MenuBar','none','ToolBar','Figure');
    FigLabel = ['Monthly Flow Duration Curves for ',...
        'ComID ',int2str(ComIDTarget),' in ',HSR,...
        ' from WY',int2str(WY1),' to WY',int2str(WY1+Ny-1)];
end
```

```
    set(gca,'XLim',[WY1-1,WY1+Ny],...
        'YLim',[10^floor(log10(min(FDC(:,im))))
10^ceil(log10(max(FDC(:,im))))]);
    title(MonthName(im),'FontSize',10,'FontWeight','bold');
    if ismember(im,[1 7])
        ylabel('Streamflow, in cubic feet per second',...
            'HorizontalAlignment','Right','FontSize',12);
    end
    if ismember(im,[10,11,12])
        xlabel('Water Year');
    end
    % Place title on plot
    if (im==1)
        ymin = 10^floor(log10(min(FDC(:,im))));
        if ymin<0.01
            ymin = 0.01;
        end
        ymax = 10^ ceil(log10(max(FDC(:,im))));
        text(WY1,10^(log10(ymax)+.35*(log10(ymax)-log10(ymin))),...
            FigLabel,'FontWeight','bold');
    end
    %
    hold on
    % Qvec is the vector of measured flows and -9999 indicators of less
    % than values, where
    % Tvec is the vector of times
    Qvec = [FDC(NdxNonZQe{im},im);-9999*ones(length(NdxZeroQe{im}),1)];
    Tvec = [WY1-1+[NdxNonZQe{im}'; NdxZeroQe{im}]];
    [tau, pval, intcpt, med slope, med data, med time yhat] = ...
        AFKenSen_v1d(Tvec,Qvec,-9999,'ne');
    %
    % Trend type is StraightLine or MovingAverage
    % Evaluating trend at a user-specifiable level
    if pval < alpha
            fprintf(1,['Month     tau     p-value     intercept    ',...
                'median slope    median data  median time\n']);
            fprintf(1,'%5s %7.5f    %7.4f    %12.4f %11.4f %14.4f %12.2f \n',...
                MoName{im},tau,pval,intcpt,med slope,med data,med time);
        switch method
            case 'Linear'
                % Plot the estimated monotonic trend
                semilogy([WY1-1,WY1+Ny],...
                    [intcpt+(WY1-1)*med slope,intcpt+(WY1-1+Ny)*med slope],...
                    'r-','LineWidth',1.5);
                %
            case 'Moving Average'
                % Compute the exponentially weighted moving average to track
trend
                S    = zeros(Ny,1); b = zeros(Ny,1);
                S(1) =  median(FDC(1:5,im));
                b(1) = (FDC(1,im)-FDC(Ny,im))/Ny;
                for i=2:Ny,
                    S(i) = a1*FDC(i,im)+(1-a1)*(S(i-1)-b(i-1));
                    b(i) = g1*(S(i)-S(i-1))+(1-g1)*b(i-1);
                end
                % Plot the double exponentially weighted moving average
                semilogy(WY1:WY1-1+Ny,S,'r-','LineWidth',1.5);
        end
```

```
10^ceil(log10(max(FDC(:,im)))))]);
        title(MonthName(im),'FontSize',10,'FontWeight','bold');
        if ismember(im,11)
            xlabel('Percentage of time indicated value was equalled or
exceeded',...
                'VerticalAlignment','Top','FontSize',12);
        end
        if ismember(im,[1 7])
            ylabel('Streamflow, in cubic feet per second',...
                'HorizontalAlignment','Right','FontSize',12);
        end
        % Place title on plot
        if (im==1)
            ymin = 10^floor(log10(min(FDC(:,im))));
            if ymin<0.01
                ymin = 0.01;
            end
            ymax = 10^ ceil(log10(max(FDC(:,im))));
            text(-3,10^(log10(ymax)+.35*(log10(ymax)-log10(ymin))),...
                FigLabel,'FontWeight','bold');
        end
end
hold off
%
```

Setup Time Series Plot

```
figure(21);clf(21);
% if-else-end labels plot according to whether or not a gage exits.
if FlagStation==1
    set(gcf,'NumberTitle','off','Name',['Trends in Monthly Flows for ',...
        'ComID ',int2str(ComIDTarget),' in ',HSR,' at gaging station ',...
        StationTarget,' based on AFinch data from WY',...
        int2str(WY1),' to WY',int2str(WY1+Ny-1)],...
        'MenuBar','none','ToolBar','Figure'),...
        FigLabel = ['Monthly Time Series for ',...
        'ComID ',int2str(ComIDTarget),' in ',HSR,' at gaging station ',...
        StationTarget,' from WY',...
        int2str(WY1),' to WY',int2str(WY1+Ny-1)];
else
    set(gcf,'NumberTitle','off','Name',['Trends in Monthly Flows for ',...
        'ComID ',int2str(ComIDTarget),' in ',HSR,...
        ' based on AFinch data from WY',...
        int2str(WY1),' to WY',int2str(WY1+Ny-1)],...
        'MenuBar','none','ToolBar','Figure'),...
            FigLabel = ['Monthly Time Series for ',...
        'ComID ',int2str(ComIDTarget),' in ',HSR,...
        ' from WY',int2str(WY1),' to WY',int2str(WY1+Ny-1)];
end
hold on
```

Plot Time Series

```
for im=1:12,
    subplot(4,3,im);
    %
    semilogy(WY1-1+NdxNonZQe{im},FDC(NdxNonZQe{im},im),'o','MarkerSize',4,...
        'MarkerFaceColor','k','MarkerEdgeColor','k');
    hold on
    % Plot a vertical dashed line from the minimum to maximum estimated
    % nonzero flow
    MinEstZeroQ = min(EstZeroQ{im}); MaxEstZeroQ = max(EstZeroQ{im});
    for iz=1:length(NdxZeroQe{im}),
        semilogy([WY1-1+NdxZeroQe{im}(iz),WY1-1+NdxZeroQe{im}(iz)],...
            [MinEstZeroQ,MaxEstZeroQ],'Color',[0 0 0],...
            'Line',':');
    end
    %           EstZeroQ{im},'+','MarkerSize',4,...
    %           'MarkerEdgeColor','k');
    % If the index vector is not empty, plot the measured monthly flows
    if ~isempty(NdxMea)
        semilogy(WY1-1+NdxNonZQm{im},max(Qm(NdxNonZQm{im},im),.2),...
            'o','MarkerSize',4,...
            'MarkerFaceColor','r','MarkerEdgeColor','k');
    end
```

```
    set(gca,'XLim',[WY1-1,WY1+Ny],...
        'YLim',[10^floor(log10(min(FDC(:,im))))
10^ceil(log10(max(FDC(:,im))))]);
    title(MonthName(im),'FontSize',10,'FontWeight','bold');
    if ismember(im,[1 7])
        ylabel('Streamflow, in cubic feet per second',...
            'HorizontalAlignment','Right','FontSize',12);
    end
    if ismember(im,[10,11,12])
        xlabel('Water Year');
    end
    % Place title on plot
    if (im==1)
        ymin = 10^floor(log10(min(FDC(:,im))));
        if ymin<0.01
            ymin = 0.01;
        end
        ymax = 10^ ceil(log10(max(FDC(:,im))));
        text(WY1,10^(log10(ymax)+.35*(log10(ymax)-log10(ymin))),...
            FigLabel,'FontWeight','bold');
    end
    %
    hold on
    % Qvec is the vector of measured flows and -9999 indicators of less
    % than values, where
    % Tvec is the vector of times
    Qvec = [FDC(NdxNonZQe{im},im);-9999*ones(length(NdxZeroQe{im}),1)];
    Tvec = [WY1-1+[NdxNonZQe{im}'; NdxZeroQe{im}]];
    [tau, pval, intcpt, med slope, med data, med time yhat] = ...
        AFKenSen v1d(Tvec,Qvec,-9999,'ne');
    %
    % Trend type is StraightLine or MovingAverage
    % Evaluating trend at a user-specifiable level
    if pval < alpha
            fprintf(1,['Month    tau    p-value    intercept    ',...
                'median_slope    median_data    median_time\n']);
            fprintf(1,'%5s %7.5f    %7.4f    %12.4f %11.4f %14.4f %12.2f \n',...
                MoName{im},tau,pval,intcpt,med slope,med data,med time);
        switch method
            case 'Linear'
                % Plot the estimated monotonic trend
                semilogy([WY1-1,WY1+Ny],...
                    [intcpt+(WY1-1)*med_slope,intcpt+(WY1-1+Ny)*med_slope],...
                    'r-','LineWidth',1.5);
                %
            case 'Moving Average'
                % Compute the exponentially weighted moving average to track
trend
                S    = zeros(Ny,1); b = zeros(Ny,1);
                S(1) =  median(FDC(1:5,im));
                b(1) = (FDC(1,im)-FDC(Ny,im))/Ny;
                for i=2:Ny,
                    S(i) = a1*FDC(i,im)+(1-a1)*(S(i-1)-b(i-1));
                    b(i) = g1*(S(i)-S(i-1))+(1-g1)*b(i-1);
                end
                % Plot the double exponentially weighted moving average
                semilogy(WY1:WY1-1+Ny,S,'r-','LineWidth',1.5);
    end
```

```
        else
            switch method
                case 'Linear'
                    semilogy(WY1+[-1 Ny],[median(FDC(:,im)),median(FDC(:,im))],...
                        'b:','LineWidth',1.5);
                case 'Moving Average'
                % Compute the simple exponentially weighted moving average
                    S(1) = median(FDC(1:5,im));
                    for i=2:Ny,
                        S(i) = a1*FDC(i-1,im) + (1-a1)*S(i-1);
                    end
                    semilogy(WY1:WY1-1+Ny,S,'b:','LineWidth',1.5);
            end
        end
end
%
```

Write out results

```
WriteOut = questdlg('Save the time series to a file?',...
    'Write Output','Save','Don''t Save','Save');

switch WriteOut
    case 'Save'
        file =
['..\HSR',THS,'\Output\FlowSeries\ComID',int2str(ComIDTarget),'.dat'];
        file = inputdlg('Path\Filename','File name',1,cellstr(file));
        fid  = fopen(file{:},'wt');
        fprintf(  1,'              Month          Flow                  \n');
        fprintf(  1,'Year  Number   Name          ft3/s       Rank       \n');
        fprintf(fid,'              Month          Flow                  \n');
        fprintf(fid,'Year  Number   Name          ft3/s       Rank       \n');

        for i=1:Ny,
            for j=1:12,
                fprintf(  1,'%4.0f  %5.0f    %6s   %8.2f   %7.2f \n',...
                    WY1-1+i,MoNumber(j),MoName{j},FDC(i,j),ranks(i,j));
                fprintf(fid,'%4.0f  %5.0f    %6s   %8.2f   %7.2f \n',...
                    WY1-1+i,MoNumber(j),MoName{j},FDC(i,j),ranks(i,j));
            end
        end
        fclose(fid);
        fprintf(1,'%s\n',['File ',file{:},' written.']);

    case 'Don''t Save'
        fprintf(1,'Time series not written to file.\n');
end
```

Clear Variables

clear rankm ranks probm probs

Appendix 26. Compute Kendall's tau Correlation Coefficient and Sen's Monotonic Trend Slope Statistic (AFKenSen)

A Matlab function that computes Kendall's tau corcoeff and associated p-value between two variables and Sen's slope estimator. Syntax: [tau, pval, intcpt, med_slope, med_data, med_time yhat] = AFKenSen(time,data,MisInd,tail) fprintf(1,'Specify criteria for one- or two-sided test.\n'); tail = input('Enter "ne", "gt", or "lt" with single quotes: ','s');

```
function [tau, pval, intcpt, med_slope, med_data, med_time_time yhat] = ...
    AFKenSen_v1d(time,data,MisInd,tail)
if nargin == 4
    Ndx = find(data~=MisInd);
    data= data(Ndx);
    time= time(Ndx);
    n   = length(Ndx);
else
    n = length(data);
    Ndx = 1:n;
end
slopes = zeros(n*(n-1)/2,1);
```

Write out results

```
WriteOut = questdlg('Save the time series to a file?',...
    'Write Output','Save','Don''t Save','Save');

switch WriteOut
    case 'Save'
        file =
['..\HSR',THS,'\Output\FlowSeries\ComID',int2str(ComIDTarget),'.dat'];
        file = inputdlg('Path\Filename','File name',1,cellstr(file));
        fid  = fopen(file{:},'wt');
        fprintf( 1,'              Month        Flow              \n');
        fprintf( 1,'Year  Number   Name       ft3/s      Rank    \n');
        fprintf(fid,'              Month        Flow              \n');
        fprintf(fid,'Year  Number   Name       ft3/s      Rank    \n');

        for i=1:Ny,
            for j=1:12,
                fprintf( 1,'%4.0f %5.0f   %6s  %8.2f  %7.2f \n',...
                    WY1-1+i,MoNumber(j),MoName{j},FDC(i,j),ranks(i,j));
                fprintf(fid,'%4.0f %5.0f   %6s  %8.2f  %7.2f \n',...
                    WY1-1+i,MoNumber(j),MoName{j},FDC(i,j),ranks(i,j));
            end
        end
        fclose(fid);
        fprintf(1,'%s\n',['File ',file{:},' written.']);

    case 'Don''t Save'
        fprintf(1,'Time series not written to file.\n');
end
```

Clear Variables

clear rankm ranks probm probs

Appendix 27. Graphical User Interface for Plotting Images of Monthly Water Yields (AFYieldAtGagesGUI)

GUI for selecting the month to display water yields at historically gaged stations in the target hydrologic subregion

```
function AFYieldAtGagesGUI v1d
%
% Position rect = [left right width (N) height (M)]
N = 410; M = 165;
%
% Create a figure
handles.fig = figure('Units','Pixel','MenuBar','none',...
    'Position',[50, 50, N, M],'NumberTitle','off',...
    'Name','Monthly Water Yields at Gaging Stations');
% Create an axis
head.text = uicontrol('style','text',...
    'String','Select Month to Display Water Yield',...
    'FontSize',12,'FontName','Arial','FontWeight','bold',...
    'ForegroundColor',[0 0 1],...
    'Position',[1 1 N M]);
%
Oct.CheckBox = uicontrol('style','radiobutton','string','October',...
    'FontSize',11,'FontWeight','bold',...
    'position',[N-405 M- 50 100 25]);
%
Nov.CheckBox = uicontrol('style','radiobutton','string','November',...
    'FontSize',11,'FontWeight','bold',...
    'position',[N-305 M- 50 100 25]);
%
Dec.CheckBox = uicontrol('style','radiobutton','string','December',...
    'FontSize',11,'FontWeight','bold',...
    'position',[N-205 M- 50 100 25]);
%
Jan.CheckBox = uicontrol('style','radiobutton','string','January',...
    'FontSize',11,'FontWeight','bold',...
    'position',[N-105 M- 50 100 25]);
%
Feb.CheckBox = uicontrol('style','radiobutton','string','February',...
    'FontSize',11,'FontWeight','bold',...
    'position',[N-405 M- 75 100 25]);
%
Mar.CheckBox = uicontrol('style','radiobutton','string','March',...
    'FontSize',11,'FontWeight','bold',...
    'position',[N-305 M- 75 100 25]);
%
Apr.CheckBox = uicontrol('style','radiobutton','string','April',...
    'FontSize',11,'FontWeight','bold',...
    'position',[N-205 M- 75 100 25]);
%
May.CheckBox = uicontrol('style','radiobutton','string','May',...
    'FontSize',11,'FontWeight','bold',...
    'position',[N-105 M- 75 100 25]);
%
Jun.CheckBox = uicontrol('style','radiobutton','string','June',...
    'FontSize',11,'FontWeight','bold',...
    'position',[N-405 M-100 100 25]);
%
Jul.CheckBox = uicontrol('style','radiobutton','string','July',...
    'FontSize',11,'FontWeight','bold',...
    'position',[N-305 M-100 100 25]);
%
Aug.CheckBox = uicontrol('style','radiobutton','string','August',...
    'FontSize',11,'FontWeight','bold',...
    'position',[N-205 M-100 100 25]);
%
Sep.CheckBox = uicontrol('style','radiobutton','string','September',...
    'FontSize',11,'FontWeight','bold',...
    'position',[N-105 M-100 100 25]);
%
```

```
VariableText.Text = uicontrol('Style','text','FontSize',12,...
    'String','Variable name of digitized data tip:',...
    'FontSize',12,'FontName','Arial','FontWeight','bold',...
    'ForegroundColor',[0 0 1],...
    'Position',[N-410,M-130,270,20],'HorizontalAlignment','right');
%
IDtipText.Text = uicontrol('Style','text','FontSize',12,...
    'String','ID Station Year of data tip:',...
    'FontSize',12,'FontName','Arial','FontWeight','bold',...
    'ForegroundColor',[0 0 1],...
    'Position',[N-410,M-160,270,20],'HorizontalAlignment','right');
%
VariableEdit.Edit = uicontrol('Style','edit','FontSize',12,...
    'String','cursor_info',...
    'Position',[N-135,M-130,120,20],'HorizontalAlignment','left');
%
Submit.PushButton = uicontrol('Style','pushbutton','FontSize',12,...
    'String','Submit',...
    'Position',[N-135,M-160,70,20],'HorizontalAlignment','center');
%
set(Oct.CheckBox,'callback',{@Oct_Callback, Oct});
set(Nov.CheckBox,'callback',{@Nov_Callback, Nov});
set(Dec.CheckBox,'callback',{@Dec_Callback, Dec});
set(Jan.CheckBox,'callback',{@Jan_Callback, Jan});
set(Feb.CheckBox,'callback',{@Feb_Callback, Feb});
set(Mar.CheckBox,'callback',{@Mar_Callback, Mar});
set(Apr.CheckBox,'callback',{@Apr_Callback, Apr});
set(May.CheckBox,'callback',{@May_Callback, May});
set(Jun.CheckBox,'callback',{@Jun_Callback, Jun});
set(Jul.CheckBox,'callback',{@Jul_Callback, Jul});
set(Aug.CheckBox,'callback',{@Aug_Callback, Aug});
set(Sep.CheckBox,'callback',{@Sep_Callback, Sep});
set(VariableEdit.Edit,'callback',{@VariableEdit_Callback, VariableEdit});
set(Submit.PushButton,'callback',{@Submit_Callback, Submit});
%
    function Oct_Callback(gcf, event_data, Oct)
        Oct.BoxStatus = get(gcf,'Value');
        assignin('base','TargetMonth',1);
        fprintf(1,'October selected.\n');
        evalin('base','AFImagePOAYield v1d');
        set(gcf,'Value',0);
    end
%
    function Nov_Callback(gcf, event_data, Nov)
        Nov.BoxStatus = get(gcf,'Value');
        assignin('base','TargetMonth',2);
        fprintf(1,'November selected.\n');
        evalin('base','AFImagePOAYield v1d');
        set(gcf,'Value',0);
    end
%
    function Dec_Callback(gcf, event_data, Dec)
        Dec.BoxStatus = get(gcf,'Value');
        assignin('base','TargetMonth',3);
        fprintf(1,'December selected.\n');
        evalin('base','AFImagePOAYield v1d');
        set(gcf,'Value',0);
    end
%
    function Jan_Callback(gcf, event_data, Jan)
        Jan.BoxStatus = get(gcf,'Value');
        assignin('base','TargetMonth',4);
        fprintf(1,'January selected.\n');
        evalin('base','AFImagePOAYield_v1d');
        set(gcf,'Value',0);
    end
%
    function Feb_Callback(gcf, event_data, Feb)
        Feb.BoxStatus = get(gcf,'Value');
        assignin('base','TargetMonth',5);
        fprintf(1,'February selected.\n');
        evalin('base','AFImagePOAYield_v1d');
        set(gcf,'Value',0);
    end
%
```

```
    function Mar Callback(gcf, event data, Mar)
        Mar.BoxStatus = get(gcf,'Value');
        assignin('base','TargetMonth',6);
        fprintf(1,'March selected.\n');
        evalin('base','AFImagePOAYield_v1d');
        set(gcf,'Value',0);
    end
%
    function Apr Callback(gcf, event data, Apr)
        Apr.BoxStatus = get(gcf,'Value');
        assignin('base','TargetMonth',7);
        fprintf(1,'April selected.\n');
        evalin('base','AFImagePOAYield v1d');
        set(gcf,'Value',0);
    end
%
    function May_Callback(gcf, event_data, May)
        May.BoxStatus = get(gcf,'Value');
        assignin('base','TargetMonth',8);
        fprintf(1,'May selected.\n');
        evalin('base','AFImagePOAYield v1d');
        set(gcf,'Value',0);
    end
%
    function Jun_Callback(gcf, event_data, Jun)
        Jun.BoxStatus = get(gcf,'Value');
        assignin('base','TargetMonth',9);
        fprintf(1,'June selected.\n');
        evalin('base','AFImagePOAYield v1d');
        set(gcf,'Value',0);
    end
%
    function Jul_Callback(gcf, event_data, Jul)
        Jul.BoxStatus = get(gcf,'Value');
        assignin('base','TargetMonth',10);
        fprintf(1,'July selected.\n');
        evalin('base','AFImagePOAYield v1d');
        set(gcf,'Value',0);
    end
%
    function Aug Callback(gcf, event data, Aug)
        May.BoxStatus = get(gcf,'Value');
        assignin('base','TargetMonth',11);
        fprintf(1,'August selected.\n');
        evalin('base','AFImagePOAYield v1d');
        set(gcf,'Value',0);
    end
%
    function Sep_Callback(gcf, event_data, Sep)
        Sep.BoxStatus = get(gcf,'Value');
        assignin('base','TargetMonth',12);
        fprintf(1,'September selected.\n');
        evalin('base','AFImagePOAYield_v1d');
        set(gcf,'Value',0);
    end
%
    function VariableEdit Callback(gcf, event data, VariableEdit)
        VariableEdit.DataTip = get(gcf,'String');
        assignin('base','DataTip',VariableEdit.DataTip);
        fprintf(1,'DataTip: %s\n',VariableEdit.DataTip);
    end
%
    function Submit_Callback(gcf, event_data, Submit)
        DataTip = evalin('base','DataTip');
        fprintf(1,'%s\n',['AFid v1d(',DataTip,')']);
        evalin('base',['AFid v1d(',DataTip,')']);
    end
end
```

Appendix 28. Plot Image of Water Yields at Historically Gaged Streams (AFImagePOAYield)

Create image of water yields in the full network over time by month for the Period of Analysis (POA)

```
fname = ['..\HSR',THS(1:2),'00\Flowlines\StationComID.csv'];
[StationAll,StationComIDAll] = textread(fname,'%s%f',...
    'delimiter',',','headerlines',1);
%
fname = ['..\',HSR,'\GagedCatchments\StationList.txt'];
StationTHS = textread(fname,'%s');
%
Ns = length(StationTHS);
StaNdxTHS = zeros(Ns,1); ComIDTHS = zeros(Ns,1);
for is = 1:Ns,
    StaNdxTHS(is) = strmatch(StationTHS(is),StationAll,'exact');
    ComIDTHS(is)  = StationComIDAll(StaNdxTHS(is));
    fprintf(1,'%4.0f  %s  %6.0f %12.0f\n',...
        is,StationTHS{is},StaNdxTHS(is),ComIDTHS(is));
end
%
% Read in station numbers and drainage areas in square miles
fname = ['..\HSR',THS(1:2),'00\Streamflow\StationDASqMi.csv'];
[StaAll,DASqMi] = textread(fname,'%s%f','delimiter',',','headerlines',1);
%
% Eliminate streamgages with indeterminate drainage areas
NdxDet = find(DASqMi>0);
StaAll = StaAll(NdxDet);
DASqMi = DASqMi(NdxDet);
%
DASqMiTHS = zeros(Ns,1);
for is = 1:Ns,
    StaNdxTHS(is) = strmatch(StationTHS(is),StaAll);
    DASqMiTHS(is) = DASqMi(StaNdxTHS(is));
    fprintf(1,'%4.0f %s %4.0f %5.2f \n',...
        is,StaAll{StaNdxTHS(is)},StaNdxTHS(is),DASqMiTHS(is));
end
%
% Determine the number of stations active in the POA
% The resulting flow lines are sorted in ascending order.
[FlowComID,ia,ib] = intersect(ComIDTHS,TrendDurationMatrix(1,1).ComIDQm(:,1));
%
Nt = length(FlowComID);
DASqMiTDM = zeros(Nt,1); StationTDM = cell(Nt,1); ComIDTDM = zeros(Nt,1);
for it=1:Nt,
    ndx           = find(FlowComID(it)==ComIDTHS);
    DASqMiTDM(it) = DASqMiTHS(ndx);
```

```
    StationTDM(it) = StationTHS(ndx);
    ComIDTDM(it)   = ComIDTHS(max(ndx));
end

%
% Drainage areas may be identified as negative if indeterminate.
Q = zeros([Ny,length(ib),12]); Y = zeros([Ny,length(ib),12]);
[d1,d2,d3] = size(Q);
% For each year in the period of analysis
for iy=1:Ny,
    % For each station with determined drainage area
    for ic=1:length(ib),
        ndx = find(TrendDurationMatrix(1,iy).ComIDQm(ib(ic),1)==ComIDTHS);
        Q(iy,ndx,:)  = TrendDurationMatrix(1,iy).ComIDQm(ib(ic),2:13);
        Y(iy,ndx,:)  = Q(iy,ndx,:)./ DASqMiTHS(ndx);
    end
end
%
h = figure('NumberTitle','off','Name',...
    'Monthly Water Yields at Gaging Stations During the Period of
Analysis',...
    'Position',[10,30,1200,900]);
h = bar3(reshape(Y(:,:,TargetMonth),d1,d2));
colormap('Jet');
shading interp
for i = 1:length(h)
    zdata = get(h(i),'Zdata');
    set(h(i),'Cdata',zdata)
    set(h,'EdgeColor','k')
end
xlabel('USGS STREAMGAGING STATION NUMBER',...
    'FontSize',12);
ylabel('YEAR OF ANALYSIS','FontSize',12);
zlabel('WATER YIELD, IN CFSM','FontSize',12);
title([MonthName{TargetMonth},...
    ' Water Yields at Streamgage Locations Operated during the Period of
Analysis',...
    ],'FontSize',12);
set(gca,'YLim',[0 Ny]);
if (Ny/5>4)
    delYr  =  5;
else
    delYr  = 10;
end
set(gca,'YTickLabel',(WY1-1):delYr:WYn);
xtick = 1:2:length(StationTDM);
set(gca,'XTick',xtick);
set(gca,'XTickLabel',StationTHS(xtick),'FontSize',7);
colorbar('location','EastOutside');
```

Appendix 29. Identify Streamgages and Gaging Activity from Image Plot (AFid)

```
function AFid_v1d(datatip)
% function AFid identifies the station water year of analysis from a
% digitized datatip commonly stored in a cursor_info type structure
StationTHS  = evalin('base','StationTHS');
WY1         = evalin('base','WY1');
Y           = evalin('base','Y');
Q           = evalin('base','Q');
TarMon      = evalin('base','TargetMonth');
MoName      = evalin('base','MoName');
DASqMiTHS   = evalin('base','DASqMiTHS');
StaHist     = evalin('base','StaHist');
fprintf(1,'%s\n',repmat('-',64,1));
fprintf(1,'                           Water     Flow     Area    Yield     Cursor
\n');
fprintf(1,' Station  Active Month  Year     cfs      mi2      cfsm     pos(3)
\n');
fprintf(1,'%s\n',repmat('-',64,1));
for i=1:length(datatip),
%     fprintf(1,'i=  %6.0f, x=  %12.4f, y=  %12.4f, z=  %12.4f\n',...
%         i,datatip(i).Position(1:3));
    % Round the x-location to the nearest integer to id the station
    StaNdx    = round(datatip(i).Position(1));
    GraphTime = round(datatip(i).Position(2));
    WY        = WY1 + GraphTime -1;
    Match = findstr(StationTHS{StaNdx},[StaHist(1,GraphTime).StaList{:}]);
    if ~isempty(Match)
        Active = 'T';
    else
        Active = 'F';
    end
    fprintf(1,'%s    %s    %s %6.0f %8.2f %8.2f %8.4f %8.4f \n',...
        StationTHS{StaNdx},Active,...
        MoName{TarMon},WY,Q(GraphTime,StaNdx,TarMon),...
        DASqMiTHS(StaNdx),Y(GraphTime,StaNdx,TarMon),...
        datatip(i).Position(3));
end
```

www.ingramcontent.com/pod-product-compliance
Lightning Source LLC
Chambersburg PA
CBHW080417290526
45791CB00008BA/2315

9 781496 133946